Say It Right
1000 Most Mispronounced Words

The **One Hour Wordpower** *series*

One Hour Wordpower

Say It Right
1000 Most Mispronounced Words

GRAHAM KING

Mandarin
in association with
The Sunday Times

A Mandarin Paperback
SAY IT RIGHT

First published in Great Britain 1994
by Mandarin Paperbacks
an imprint of Reed Consumer Books Ltd
Michelin House, 81 Fulham Road, London SW3 6RB
and Auckland, Melbourne, Singapore and Toronto

Reprinted 1994 (three times)

A CIP catalogue record for this title
is available from the British Library
ISBN 0 7493 1877 5

Printed and bound in Great Britain
by Cox & Wyman Ltd, Reading, Berks

Contents

Acknowledgements

The following works have been consulted and thanks are due to their authors and publishers:

Bryson, Bill. *Mother Tongue*. Penguin, 1990.

Claiborne, Robert. *Life and Times of the English Language*. Bloomsbury, 1990.

Collins English Dictionary. HarperCollins, 1992.

Coombes, Allen. *Dictionary of Plant Names*. Collingridge, 1987.

Crystal, David. *Encyclopedia of Language*. Cambridge University Press, 1987.

Dear, I. C. B. (Ed). *Oxford English*. Oxford University Press, 1986.

Honey, John. *Does Accent Matter?* Faber & Faber, 1989.

Oxford English Dictionary – concise and complete editions.

Pointon, G. E. (Ed). *BBC Pronouncing Dictionary of British Names*. Oxford University Press, 1990.

Potter, Simeon. *Our Language*. Penguin, 1959.

Schoonmaker, Frank. *Encyclopedia of Wine*. Hastings House, 1976.

Tripp, Edward. *Handbook of Classical Mythology*. Baker, 1972.

Upton, Sandeson & Widdowson. *Word Maps*. Croom Helm, 1987.

Wells, J. C. *Pronunciation Dictionary*, Longmans, 1990.

Whitten, W. and Whitaker, F. *Good and Bad English*. Newnes, 1950.

Witherspoon, A. *Common Errors in English*. Barnes & Noble, 1959.

Consultant on linguistics: Paul Coggle, Senior Lecturer in German, University of Kent at Canterbury.

Introduction

Consider this. At a very early age a child must learn how to pump breath at varying velocities through the larynx, to store it and release it and then to manipulate it by complex movements of the tongue, lips, teeth and cheeks. When the child has accomplished this and has learned to do it at speed, it is called speech.

But that's only the beginning. As the child grows up it learns how to turn speech into communication. If the child lives in an English-speaking environment, this communication system, or language, is called English. The child then learns to read and this is where the fun really begins!

The learner then has to cope with the many logic-defying aspects of English pronunciation: why, for example, words like *victuals*, *chough*, *forecastle* and *trait* are pronounced quite differently from what their spelling suggests.

Then there are the multitudinous ways in which the same sound is represented by different letter combinations: *ship*, *sure*, *champagne*, *ocean*, *ambitious* and *passion* are all words that use the **'sh'** sound. Why is the **'th'** in *thy* pronounced softer than the **'th'** in *thigh*? Why does the **'ng'** in *finger* sound different to the **'ng'** in *singer*? Welcome to the mysteries of English pronunciation.

Of course, English isn't the only language to contain irrationality (French expresses the **'o'** sound in at least eight different spellings: *au, aut, aux, eau, eaux, o, os* and *ot*) but it is more consistently quirky than most.

This is perhaps why the teaching of English generally, and pronunciation in particular, is rarely out of the headlines. The most recent debate storms around the teaching of that variety of speech called Received Pronunciation, which its opponents regard as an homogenising exercise designed to cleanse the

7

population of its accents and dialects.

The fact is that Received Pronunciation is our best effort at achieving a consistent national spoken language that is clear and unambiguous wherever it is heard. It is primarily about pronunciation with the stresses and nuances in the right places, and has very little to do with social class, accent or dialect. A word pronounced correctly, whatever the accent used, is simply that; and if *gibbet* is pronounced **GIB-ut** and not **JIB-ut**, it is wrong whether it's spoken in Received Pronunciation, Scots, Scouse, Cockney or West Country.

In real life, to be able to pronounce words as they are intended to be pronounced, or to be 'well-spoken' to use a genteel term, is clearly an asset: it indicates to most hearers that the speaker is informed, discerning and self-confident. And, increasingly in the competitive employment market-place, it gives the careful speaker a decided edge over a candidate who is at odds with correct pronunciation.

Say It Right is a mere dip into our linguistic cauldron, a fascinating brew of words bubbling with absurdities, change and glorious confusion. But in its pages you are likely to find most of the words and names used in everyday speech that are lying in wait to trip us up.

Pronunciation Guide

The most accurate guide to the correct pronunciation of a word or name is the International Phonetic Alphabet (IPA) which, with its fifty or so symbols, will tell anyone, anywhere, in any language, how to say a word or name in any other language. All good dictionaries now feature the IPA.

If you turn to page 38 you will see the IPA explained. You will also see why it is not used as a guide for this book. First you would need to spend some time memorising the symbols. Second, *Say It Right* is a mini-dictionary of words that are frequently mispronounced and it is intended for English speakers who are, at the very least, acquainted with the sounds of simple letter combinations like STY, HAY, GO, BOO, and AK. So in the spirit of the *One Hour Wordpower* books to keep things simple, our pronunciation guide is built on basic groups of letters:

acoustic	ah-KOO-stik
demise	dem-EYES
privy	PRIV-ee

Still, there are a few traps. Words ending in ... *y* may be pronounced differently:

early	ER-lee	(*the 'long e' sound*)
layby	LAY-by	(*the 'long i' sound*)

To make the difference clear, the 'long e' sound will always be indicated by **'ee'** to rhyme with *glee*, and the 'long i' sound by a **'y'**, to rhyme with *eye*.

One of the most common mistakes in pronunciation is to stress the wrong syllable. Most words have a strong stress on a single syllable, although a good many multi-syllable words have a secondary, or weaker stressed syllable, as well. In this book the strong stress

9

is capitalised, and the weak stress is underlined:

crescendo	kreh-SHEN-doh
repartee	rep-uh-TEE
requiescat	<u>rek</u>-wih-ESS-kut
sinecure	SIN-ih-<u>kyoor</u>

The words and names that trip us up with embarrassing frequency are undoubtedly those imported from other countries, especially France. Apart from having to know where the stress goes, English speakers also have to cope with French nasalisation (horrible word, but appropriate). Nasalisation results in losing the end of a word in a combination of a sneer and a snort, which doesn't come easy to those who regard any noise emanating from the nose as distasteful or as the sign of a bad cold.

If you are one of those who needs to use such words in your conversation but who lacks the confidence to say them, this book should help you.

One of these foreign sounds is the one that combines an 's' and a 'z' resulting in the softly sibilant **'s'** in *leisure* and *vision*. This sound is indicated by the letter combination **zh**:

protégé	PROT-eh-zhay
adjunct	AD-zhunkt
mélange	muh-LARNZH

The more difficult sound is the nasalisation already referred to, required to pronounce correctly words like *vin* and names like *blanc de blancs*. Most people manage to produce a sound like **vahng** for the former, which isn't too bad, and **blonk duh blonk** for the latter, which all but pedants find acceptable. But if you wish to do better you could try to nasalise the ends of the syllables, and to indicate where this is required we have used the following device:

10

> **blanc de blancs**   blah(n) duh blah(n)

or, with the ultimately nasal-sounding word:

> **embonpoint**   arh(n)-bor(n)-pwah(n)

In short, the (n) indicates that the preceding vowel sounds should be followed by an **'ng'** sound that somehow gets lost up the nose. If you listen to a fluent French speaker, or to a language tape, you should get the idea fairly quickly.

Finally, you will frequently come across **'uhl'** in the listings:

> **risible**   RIS-i-buhl
> **vegetable**   VEJ-tah-buhl

What we are trying to do here is to ask you not to make a big deal out of the *'ble'* by saying Vej-tah-bool, but to treat it with dismissive brevity.

1000 Most Mispronounced Words

abalone	<u>ab</u>-uh-LOW-nih
abattoir	AB-ah-twar
abdomen	AB-duh-men (*but to confuse us, many doctors still use the older* ab-DOH-men)
abdominal	ab-DOM-i-nal
abseil	AB-syl
abstemious	ab-STEE-mih-us
abysmal	a-BIZZ-muhl; *also* a-BISS-muhl
abyss	a-BISS
accent	AK-sent
accidie	AK-sid-ee
acclimate	ak-KLY-mayt
accolade	AK-oh-<u>layd</u>; *also* <u>ak</u>-oh-LAYD
accoutrement	ah-KOO-treh-mah(n)
acerbic	uh-SER-bik
acerbity	uh-SER-bit-ee
acoustic	ah-KOO-stik
acumen	AK-kyoo-men
adage	AD-ij
adagio	ah-DARD-joh
adept	ad-EPT
adherent	ad-HEER-ent
adieu	ah-dyur
adjunct	AD-zhunkt
admirable	AD-mir-u-buhl
admiralty	AD-mi-rul-tee
adobe	ad-DOH-bee; *also* ad-DOH-bay
adult	AD-ult; *but* ad-ULT *is also common*
adumbrate	AD-um-<u>brayt</u>
adversary	AD-vuh-s'ree
advertisement	ad-VERT-iz-<u>ment</u>
aegis	EED-jis
aeon	EE-uhn

aesthetic	es-THET-ik
affectation	aff-ek-TAY-shun
aficionado	ah-<u>feess</u>-yuh-NAR-doh
aged	ayjd, *except for* AY-jid *when used in the sense,* '*caring for the aged*'
agent provocateur	AH-zhar (n) <u>prov</u>-ok-uh-TOOR
aggrandize	ag-GRAN-dyz; *rarely* AG-gran-dyz
aide-mémoire	ayd-mem-WAH
akimbo	ah-KIM-boh

The Shifting Accent

If an elderly person pronounces a word differently from the pronunciation familiar to you, don't regard it as a sign of senility; the sounds of many words have changed markedly over the past couple of generations. It is not, of course, surprising to find that a word is pronounced differently now from what it was in Dr Johnson's day: *ache* (the noun), formerly *aytch*, is now pronounced **ayk**; *niche* was for two centuries called <u>nitch</u> until recently when a changeover to **neesh** occurred, to trot out just two examples. More surprising, however, is the discovery that many pronunciations have changed in the fifty years since the end of World War II. Most of the changes result from a shifting accent, or the movement of stress from one syllable to another. Here are some typical samples; first, with pronunciations recommended by at least three authoritative dictionaries of the time (1935–50), followed by the usual pronunciation today.

WORD	FORMERLY	TODAY
abdomen	ab-DOH-men	AB-doh-men
aggrandize	AG-gran-dyz	ag-GRAN-dyz

---

albeit	awl-BEE-it
albumen	AL-byoo-mun
alias	AY-li-us
allegory	AL-leh-gur-ee
almond	AR-mund
altruism	AL-troo-ism
aluminium	al-yoo-MIN-i-um (*not to be confused with the American* al-OO-min-um)
alumni	uh-LUM-ny

badinage	bad-in-AYJ	BAD-in-ayj
bas-relief	bass-re-leef	bar-rih-leef
encore	en-KOR	AH(N)-kor
farrago	fuh-RAY-goh	fur-RAR-goh
geyser	GAY-zer	GEE-zer
leeward	LOO-ward	LEE-wud
pejorative	PE-jor-a-tiv	pih-JOR-uh-tiv
tirade	tih-RAYD	ty-RAYD
tourniquet	torn-i-ket	torn-i-kay

There is also the group of words that includes *indisputable, inexplicable, inextricable* and *inhospitable*. Their pronunciation probably changed simply because people could not get their tongues around the recommended sound:

FORMERLY	TODAY
in-DIS-pyoo-tuh-buhl	in-dis-PYOO-tuh-buhl
in-EKS-plik-uh-buhl	in-eks-PLIK-uh-buhl
in-EKS-trik-uh-buhl	in-eks-TRIK-uh-buhl
in-HOS-pit-ah-buhl	in-hos-PIT-ah-buhl

Confusingly, *inexorable* retains the original **in-EKS-ruh-buhl**!

ambience	AHM-byee-arns
amenable	ah-MEEN-uh-buhl
amenity	ah-MEEN-it-ee
amok	ah-MUK
amoral	ay-MOR-al
amour	ah-MOOR
anachronism	an-NAK-ron-ism
analgesic	an-al-JEE-zik
analagous	ah-NAL-o-gus
anemone	ah-NEM-uh-nee
anaesthetist	an-EESS-thuh-<u>tist</u>
angina	an-JY-nuh
animadvert	<u>an</u>-im-ad-VERT
annihilate	an-NY-il-<u>ayt</u>
anomalous	ah-NOM-al-us
anomie	AN-oh-mih
anonymity	<u>an</u>-oh-NIM-i-tee
antipodes	an-TIP-oh-dees
antiquary	ANT-tih-kwar-ee
antithesis	an-TITH-ih-<u>sis</u>
apparatus	ap-puh-RAY-tus
apartheid	ah-PART-tayt
aperçu	ap-er-syoo; *also* ap-er-soo
aperitif	ah-per-i-TEEF
apocryphal	ah-POK-rif-uhl
apostasy	uh-POS-tuh-see
apotheosis	ah-POTH-ee-oh-<u>sis</u>
apophthegm	AP-puh-them
applicable	AP-lik-uh-buhl
appliqué	ap-PLEE-kay
apposite	AP-uz-it
appurtenance	ah-PER-tuh-nans
après-ski	ap-ray-skee
a priori	ay-pree-OR-eye
apropos	<u>ap</u>-pruh-POH
arbitrary	AR-bit-rah-ree *or* AR-bit-ree
Arctic	ARK-tik
argot	AR-goh

armoire	arm-WAR
arpeggio	ar-PEJ-yoh
arraign	ar-RAYN
arriviste	ar-rih-VEEST
artisan	ART-ih-zan *is preferred to* art-ih-ZAN
art nouveau	ar-noo-voh
asinine	ASS-ih-nyn
asphalt	ASS-falt, *but* ASH-felt *is quite common*
assiduous	as-SID-you-us
assignation	as-sig-NAY-shun
assuage	as-SWAYJ
Athenaeum	ath-en-EE-um
atrophy	AT-roh-fee
attaché	ah-TASH-ay
au fait	oh-FAY
au naturel	oh-natch-yoo-REL
au pair	oh-PAIR
automaton	or-TOM-uh-ton
autopsy	OR-tup-see
auxiliary	orgs-ZIL-yoo-ree
avant-garde	av-vah(n)-GARD
avoirdupois	av-wuh-duh-PWAHR
awry	or-RY
baccalaureate	bak-uh-LOH-ray-at
baccarat	BAKKA-rah
badinage	BAD-in-arj
baguette	bag-ET
banal	buh-NARL; *alternatively,* buh-NAL
bar mitzah	bar-MITZ-vuh
bas relief	bar rih-leef
bathos	BAY-thos
baton	BAT-uhn
bayou	BY-ooh
behemoth	bih-HEE-moth
beige	bayzh

17

BBC-Speak

A handful of linguists at the British Broadcasting Corporation help maintain the BBC's reputation as the fountainhead of correct English pronunciation. The Pronunciation Unit of the BBC is headed by Graham Pointon and it handles some 200 queries a week – words, names, place-names, names of products – from BBC staff eager to say it right.

The foundation of the BBC's enunciation is what is known as Received Pronunciation (RP), a standardised, southern-based, upper-classish accent which was all a listener heard until the rich Yorkshire tones of Wilfred Pickles broke the mould in the 1940s. Although regional accents are now *de rigueur*, the Corporation remains obsessed with correct articulation, so it is not surprising that the population looks to it for guidance on pronunciation.

The BBC, in turn, listens in on Britain, constantly modifying and updating its pronunciation styles. Compare, for example, these recommendations by its original Advisory Committee on Spoken English in 1926:

WORD	1926	TODAY
balcony	bal-KOH-nee	BAL-koh-nee
decade	DEK-ayd	deh-KAYD
profile	proh-FEEL	PROH-fyl
secretive	sek-REE-tiv	SEE-kret-iv
suave	swayve	SWAR-ve
vitamin	VY-tah-min	VIT-uh-min

benign	bi-NYN
beret	BEH-ray
berserk	buh-SERK *or* buh-ZERK
bespoke	bih-SPOKE (*to rhyme with* **oak**)
bête noire	bet-NWAR
bijou	BEE-zhoo
binary	BY-nah-ree
bisque	bisk, *but often* beesk
bitumen	BIT-choo-mun
bizarre	biz-ZARR
blasé	BLAH-zay
blessed	blest *is correct for forms of the verb, but when used as an adjective and especially as a noun ('The blessed have seen the light') it is often* BLESS-id
bodega	boh-DEG-uh
bona fide	BOH-nuh FY-deh
bouffant	BOO-fah(n)
bouillabaisse	boo-ee-yuh-BES
bouquet	book-KAY
bourgeois	BOOR-zhwar
bourgeoisie	boor-zhwar-ZEE
boutonnière	boo-ton-YAIR
bovine	BOH-vyn
braggadocio	brag-uh-DOHT-chi-oh
brasserie	BRASS-ree
bravado	bruh-VAR-doh
bravura	brav-YOOR-ah
breccia	BRET-chee-uh
brochure	BROH-shoor (broh-SHOOR *in the US*)
brooch	brohch (*to rhyme with* **coach**)
brougham	BROO-um
brouhaha	BROO-hah-hah
brusque	broosk
brut	broot
budgerigar	BUD-jer-ee-gah
buffet	BOOF-fay
bulwark	BOOL-wuk

19

Baffling Botanicals

If you're a weekend gardener you have probably noticed the resigned half-smile on the faces of nursery assistants when you ask for a plant, as in: 'Oh, Miss, can I have two of those reebs and that nice big symbidium over there?' Snigger, snigger. But no more! Here's how to say it right with the flowers.

acer – AY-ser
aconitum – a-kon-EE-tum
aesculus – EYS-koo-lus
aloe – AY-loh
aloysia – a-loh-ISS-ee-uh
antirrhinum – an-tih-RY-num
aponogeton – a-pon-a-GAY-tun
aubrieta – oh-BREE-shuh
calendula – kah-LEN-dyoo-luh
callistriche – kah-LEE-tri-kee
cassiope – kah-SEE-oh-pee
ceanothus – see-ah-NOH-thus
chanomeles – ky-no-MAY-lees
chamaecyparis – kuh-my-KUH-paris
cheiranthus – kuh-RAN-thus
clematis – KLEM-uh-tis
corydalis – koh-RID-ih-lis
cotinus – KOH-tin-us
cupressocyparis – kyoo-PRESS-oh-kuh-
  paris
cupressus – kyoo-PRESS-us
cyananthus – kee-an-AN-thus
cymbidium – kim-BID-yee-um
cytisus – SIT-tis-sus
deutzia – DOYTS-ee-ah
euonymus – yoo-ON-ih-mus

euphorbia – yuh-FOR-bee-uh
ficus – FEE-kus
fuchsia – FYOO-shuh
gunnera – GUN-uh-rah
gypsophila – jip-SOF-ee-luh
hebe – HEE-bee
hypericum – hy-PER-ih-kum
ilex – EY-leks
impatiens – im-PAY-shee-ens
kalanchoe – kuh-LAN-koh-ee
lobelia – lo-BEEL-yee-ah
malus – MAR-lus
montbretia – mun-BREE-shee-ah
narcissus – nar-SISS-us
nigella – ny-GEL-luh, *but increasingly*, ny-
   DJEL-luh
origanum – uh-RIG-un-um
paeonia – py-ON-yee-uh
penstemon – pen-STEE-mun
picea – PY-kee-ah
pieris – PEE-eer-is
pittosporum – pih-TOSS-per-um
polygonatum – pol-ee-gon-ART-um
rhus – russ
ribes – RY-beez
sedum – SEE-dum
spiraea – spih-REE-uh
syringa – sih-RING-gah
verbena – ver-BAY-nuh
vinca – VING-kuh
weigela – WY-gee-luh, *but alternatively*
   wih-JEE-luh
yucca – YUH-kuh

bureaucracy	<u>byoo</u>-OK-ruh-see
cabal	kuh-BAL (*to rhyme with* **shall**)
cache	kash
cachet	kah-SHAY
cachou	KASH-ooh
cadre	KARD-uh; *sometimes* KARD-ruh
café au lait	<u>kaff</u>-ay-oh-LAY
calliope	kal-EYE-uh-pee
calumny	KAL-um-nee
camaraderie	<u>kam</u>-ar-AD-er-ee
campanile	kam-puh-NEE-lih
canard	kan-NARD
cantabile	kan-TAR-bih-lay
cappuccino	<u>kappa</u>-CHEE-noh
carburettor	<u>karb</u>-yuh-RETT-uh (KAR-boo-ray-tuh *in US*)
carcanet	KAR-kuh-net
caryatid	karri-AY-tid
casuistry	KAS-yoo-is-tree
catalogue raisonné	KAT-uh-log <u>ray</u>-zorn-nay
cause célèbre	KORZ seh-LEB-ruh
ceilidh	KAY-lih
cello	chello
celt, celtic	kelt, KEL-tik (*but the Scottish soccer team is* SEL-tik *as all Scots know*)
centrifugal	sen-TRIF-yug-uhl, *but just as widely heard is* sen-trih-FYOO-gul
cerebral	SER-ih-brool (ser-EE-brool *in the US*)
cervical	SER-vik-uhl, ser-VY-kuhl
chagrin	SHAH-grin
chaise-longue	shayzh-lor(ng)
chalet	SHAL-lay
chameleon	kam-EE-lih-<u>un</u>
chamois	SHAM-war *for the animal*; SHAM-ee *for the leather used for cleaning*
chancre	SHAN-ker

22

chaos, chaotic	KAY-os; kay-OT-ik
chapati	chuh-PAT-ee; also chuh-PAR-tih
chaperon,	
chaperone	SHAP-uh-rohn
charade	shuh-RARD
charcuterie	shar-KOO-tree
charge d'affaires	shar-zhay duh-FAIR
charlatan	SHAR-luh-tan
chasm	KAZ-um
chauffeur	SHOH-fuh
chemise	shuh-MEEZ
chiaroscuro	ky-uh-rus-KYOO-roh
chic	sheek
chicanery	shih-KAY-ner-ee
chiffonier	shiff-uh-NEER
chignon	SHEE-nyon
chimera	KIM-er-uh
chinoiserie	sheen-WAHR-zuh-ree
chiropodist	kih-ROP-oh-dist
chiropractor	KY-ruh-prak-tor
chough	chuff (*the bird*)
chrysalis	KRIS-ah-lis
chutzpah	HOOT-spah
cicada	sih-KAR-duh
cicatrice	SIK-a-triss
Cinque Ports	singk ports
circa	SER-kuh
cirrhosis	sih-ROH-sis
clandestine	klan-DES-tin
cliché	KLEE-shay
clique	kleek
cloisonné	KLWAR-zoh-nay
cloth	kloth, *not* klorth
coalesce	koh-uh-LES
coccyx	KOK-siks
codicil	KOH-dih-sil
cognisance	KOG-nih-zans
cognoscenti	kog-nuh-SHENT-ih

23

Class, Region and Accent

Many people confuse correctness of pronunciation with a classy accent. The truth is that a word is pronounced correctly or incorrectly and accents have little to do with it except to contribute a variety of phonetic flavourings to our speech.

But it is also true that despite the erosion of the old rigid British class system, most traditional accents are alive and well, whether socially or regionally derived. In his book, *Mother Tongue*, Bill Bryson muses that a sophisticated computer could probably locate where any English-speaking person lived, with an accuracy of a few miles, by asking the person to pronounce just ten words: **balm, bomb, cart, caught, cot, good, horse, house, oil** and **water**.

As far as class is concerned, Britain still maintains some sturdy prejudices about speech.

coiffeur, coiffure	KWAH-fyoor
colander	KULL-un-duh
combative	KUM-bat-iv
combine	kom-BYN (verb); KOM-byn (*harvester*)
comely	KUM-lee
communiqué	kom-MYOO-ni-kay
comparable	KOM-pruh-buhl
complacent	kom-PLAY-sent
complaisant	kom-PLAY-zunt
comptroller	kon-TROLL-er
concerto	kon-CHER-toh
concupiscence	kon-KYOO-pih-sens
conduit	KON-dyoo-it

Leading linguist Professor John Honey describes the results of experiments over several years on how the population at large regards certain accents and their owners. Regardless of their own background and accent, respondents overwhelmingly voted RP (Received Pronunciation) as the most pleasant, beautiful and desirable of them all. The rest fell roughly into the following league table (those below sixth position are not in correct order):

1 Received Pronunciation (BBC English)
2 Educated Scottish
3 Educated Welsh and Irish
4 Yorkshire
5 West Country
6 Tyneside Geordie

then Belfast, Birmingham, Cockney, Glaswegian, Indian and West Indian, Scouse.

confidante	<u>kon</u>-fih-DARNT
congeries	kon-JEER-eez
congratulatory	kun-GRAT-yuh-<u>layt</u>-ree
connoisseur	KON-iss-er
consommé	<u>kon</u>-som-MAY
constable	kun-stuh-buhl
consummate	KON-summ-at
contemplative	kon-TEMP-luh-tiv
contrary	KON-truh-ree (*opposed*);
	kon-TRAIR-ee (*obstinate*)
controversy	KON-troh-ver-see
conversant	kon-VER-sunt
coq au vin	KOK-oh-var(n)
cordon bleu	KOR-do(n) blehr

cornucopia	korn-yuh-KOH-pee-ah
corpus delicti	kor-pus deh-LIK-ty
corral	kuh-RARL
cortège	KOR-tayzh
coterie	KOH-tuh-ree
coup de grâce	KOO-dah-grahs
coup d'état	KOO-day-tahr
coupé	koo-PAY
courteous	KURT-yus
courtesan	kor-tih-ZAN
couscous	koos-koos
covert	KUV-it
covey	KUV-ee
coxswain	KOK-sun
crèche	kraysh
crescendo	kreh-SHEN-doh
crochet	KROH-shay
croûtons	kroo-TOH(N)
crudités	KROO-duh-tay
cuisine	kwee-ZEEN
cupola	KYOO-puh-lah
curettage	KYOOR-ih-tarzh
curriculum vitae	koo-RIK-yoo-lum VEET-ay
cynosure	SIN-uh-shoor
czar	zahr
dachshund	DAKS-hoond
dais	DAY-is
débâcle	day-BARK-ul
debris	DAY-bree; *also* DEB-ree
debut	DAY-byoo; *also* DEH-byoo
debutante	DEB-yoo-tarnt
decade	DEK-ayd
décolletage	day-kol-TARZH
decor	DAY-kor
decorous	DEK-uh-rus
decrease	dih-KREESS (*verb*); DEE-kreess (*noun*)

decree nisi	dih-KREE NY-zy
defect	DEE-fekt (*noun*); dih-FEKT (*verb*)
déjà vu	day-zhah-voo
deleterious	del-uh-TEER-rih-us
demesne	dih-MAYN
demise	dih-MYS
demonstrable	dih-MON-struh-buhl
dénouement	day-NOO-mah(n)
depilatory	dih-PIL-uh-tree
deprecate	DEP-rih-kayt
derisory	dih-RY-suh-ree
déshabille	day-zhuh-BEE
despicable	des-PIK-uh-buhl
desultory	DES-ult-ree
détente	day-TARNT
diámenté	dy-uh-MEN-tee
dichotomy	dih-KOT-oh-mee
dilate	dy-LAYT
dilatory	DIL-uh-tree
dilettante	dil-ih-TARNT-ih
diphtheria	dif-THEER-ee-ah
diphthong	DIF-thong
dirndl	DERN-duhl
disciplinary	DIS-ih-plin-ree
disciplinarian	dis-i-plin-AIR-i-an
discreet	dis-KREET
discrete	dis-KREET
disparage	dis-PAR-idj
disparate	DIS-prit
dissect	dih-SEKT *is preferred to the recently fashionable* dy-SEKT
dissent	dis-SENT
diuretic	di-yoo-RET-ik
divers	DY-verz
diverse	dy-VERSS
doctrinal	DOK-trih-nul *or* dok-TRY-nul
dolce vita	dolt-shih-VEE-tuh
double entendre	doo-blah(n)-TARN-druh

27

douche	doosh
doughty	DOW-tee
dynasty	DIN-us-tee
dysentery	DIS-un-tree
dyspepsia	dis-PEP-sih-uh

Dialects

From a global viewpoint, British English is just one of many varieties of the English language, alongside North American English, Caribbean English, Australian English and so on. In Britain alone, some authorities put the number of dialects as high as forty, but perhaps a dozen might be nearer the mark, including Scots, Irish, Welsh, West Country, Yorkshire, Geordie and Cockney. Furthermore, each dialect subdivides into a number of accents. It's all very confusing, so first let's answer the question: what is a dialect and what is an accent?

Somewhat simply, an accent has to do with the way words are pronounced. To the alert ear, accents give clues to the speaker's environment, background and education.

A dialect, on the other hand, is a more obvious giveaway. Apart from pronunciation differences, a dialect will feature grammatical and usage variations and include idioms unique to that dialect. Different words will crop up, too, that you'll hear nowhere else. **Frit**, for example. In parts of England it means 'frightened', and when Mrs Thatcher uttered it in a Commons debate some years ago, millions of people heard the word for the very first time. But it still survives in Lincolnshire, where Mrs Thatcher was born.

ebullient	ih-BUL-yent (*to rhyme with dull*)
Ecce Homo	EK-eh-HO-mo
eccentric	ek-SEN-trik
éclair	ay-KLAIR
eclectic	ek-LEK-tik
effete	ih-FEET
efficacious	<u>ef</u>-ih-KAY-shus
efficacy	EFF-ih-<u>kuh</u>-see
egalitarian	ih-<u>gal</u>-ih-TAIR-ee-un
egregious	ih-GREE-jus
eisteddfod	ey-STEDTH-fod
either	*By far the preferred pronunciation is* ey-thuh (*and* ny-thuh *for 'neither'*). EE-thuh *and* NEE-thuh *are more common in the US*
élan	ay-LAR(N)
elegiac	el-ih-JY-uk
élite	ay-LEET

Embolalia

'*Embolalia, you know . . . like, well, ah, it's sort of, uh, narmean?*' Exactly. Call them what you will: filler words, stammerings, vacuities, parenthetic phrases – we all use them in our speech and rather wish we didn't. There are two schools of thought on embolalia; one is for eradication, the other is for tolerance.

The tolerant school has a point, which is that fillers give the speaker extra thinking time, paper over awkward silences, add colour and rhythm to speech and provide clues about the speaker's knowledge (or lack of it) of what he or she is talking about. While perfect, precise enunciation can sound distant and forbidding, too much verbal padding can be quite irritating; but before you start casting stones, check a tape recording of your own speech. Y'know, narmean?

29

embonpóint	arh(n)-bor(n)-pwah(n)
embouchure	arh(n)-boo-SHOOR
embryonic	em-bree-ON-ik
eminence grise	ay-min-arh(n)s-GRIZ
emphysema	<u>em</u>-fih-SEEM-uh
enclave	EN-klayv
encore	ONG-kor
endive	EN-dyv
enfant terrible	arh(n)-fah(n)-teh-REEB-luh
en masse	arh(n)-MASS
ennui	AHR(N)-wuih, *but* ON-wee *will do*
ensemble	arh(n)-SAR(N)-bluh, *but* on-SOM-buhl *is quite acceptable in English*
ensilage	EN-sih-<u>lij</u>
en suite	ahr(n)-sweet
entente	ahr(n)-TARNT
entourage	<u>on</u>-too-RARZH
entrée	ARH(N)-tray
entrepreneur	on-<u>truh</u>-pruh-NER
environs	en-VY-runs

When ER is AR

Why is **clerk** pronounced **klark?** and **Derby** pronounced **Darby?** For the answer we have to go back to pre-Elizabethan times, when it was standard to pronounce 'er' words as 'ar': '*That person wants his soup served now*' would have sounded like '*That parson wants his soup sarved now.*' By the end of the eighteenth century, however, most of the 'er' words were pronounced as spelt with (naturally) some unexplainable exceptions like **clerk**, **Derby**, **sergeant** and, of course, **Berkshire** and **Hertford**.

epiphany	ih-PIFF-uh-nee
epitome	ih-PIT-uh-mee
equitable	EK-wit-uh-buhl
equivocate	eh-KWIV-uh-kayt
erudite	EHR-ruh-dyt
eschew	ess-CHEW
escritoire	ESS-krih-TWAHR
esoteric	es-uh-TER-tik
espionage	ESS-pih-uh-narzh
esprit de corps	es-pree-dih-KOR
etcetera	et-SET-er-uh
etiquette	ET-ih-ket *is preferred to* et-ih-KET
exacerbate	ig-ZASS-uh-bayt
execrable	EKS-ih-krah-buhl
exegesis	eks-ih-JEE-sis
ex gratia	eks-GRAY-shuh
exigency	EKS-id-jen-see, *but perhaps because this pronunciation is difficult, it is common to hear it as* ig-SIDJ-in-see
expatiate	eks-PAY-shih-it
expletive	EKS-plih-tiv
expurgate	EKS-per-gayt
extempore	ek-STEM-pree
extirpate	EKS-tuh-payt
extraordinary	eks-TROR-din-ree
façade	fuh-SARD
faeces	FEE-sees
fait accompli	fet-uh-KOM-plee
falcon	FORL-kun
farrago	fuh-RAR-go
Fascist	FASH-ist
faux pas	foh-PAR
febrile	FEE-bryl
fecund	FEE-kund
feral	FEER-ul *or* FEH-rul
fiancé, fiancée	*Both are pronounced* fee-OHN-say
fifth	fif-th (*do you sound both 'f's?*)

F for TH

'No, James, it's not free, it's three: t-h-r-e-e!'
Thousands of parents are driven to correct their
children's pronunciation of the **'th'** sound in
words like **teeth**, **truth**, **youth** and **month**
which come out like **teef**, **troof**, **yoof** and **munf**.
The transposition is of course a feature of
Cockney: *'Fings aren't what you fink vey are'*, in
which the **'th'**, in words such as **they**, **the** and
with is further modified to **vey**, **vuh** and **wiv**.
Curiously, although there are perhaps a couple
of thousand words in English containing the **'th'**
sounds, it is a phoneme almost entirely absent
from other languages.

finance	fih-NANTS *has a slight edge over* FY-nants
finesse	fih-NESS
fjord	FEE-yord
flaccid	FLAK-sid, *but* FLAS-sid *is a common alternative*
flambé	FLAH(N)-bay
fleur-de-lis	fler-duh-LEES
forbade	for-BAD
forecastle	FOHK-sul
forehead	FOR-rid (*to rhyme with horrid*)
formidable	FOR-mid-uh-buhl *or* for-MID-uh-buhl
forte	FOR-tay
foyer	FOR-yay
fracas	FRAK-ar
frappé	frah-PAY
Frau	frow (*to rhyme with how*)
Fräulein	FROY-lyn
frequent	FREE-kwent (*adjective*); frih-KWENT (*verb*)

fricassee	FRIK-uh-see; *less often* frik-ah-SEE
frisson	FREE-soh(n)
fruit-de-mer	<u>fwee</u>-duh-MAIR
fungi	*The preferred form is* FUNG-gee, *but the two alternatives,* FUNG-gy *and* FUN-jee, *are also in common use*
furore	fyoo-ROR-eh
fuselage	FYOO-suh-lidj *or* FYOO-suh-lahzh
gaffe	gaff
gallant	GALL-lant (*adjective*); guh-LANT (*noun*)
garage	GAR-rarzh *is preferred to* GAR-ridj (but the US gur-ARZH is catching on)
gauche	gohsh
gazebo	guh-ZEE-boh
gazpacho	gaz-PATCH-oh

Genre

'Sir,' began a recent letter to *The Times*, 'the pronunciation of certain awkward but useful words prompts me to ask about *genre*. It is almost impossible to pronounce it in an English sentence without sounding pedantic or superior – or feeling a bit embarrassed. But it is very useful and there does not seem to be an alternative in English. Or is there?' Type? Style, sort, brand, variety, class, category, school? No, perhaps it might be smarter to learn how to pronounce it with poise and pizzazz. Try **ZHARN-ruh**, sounding the **ZH** like the **'s'** in **pleasure** and keeping the **'ruh'** as a swallowed afterthought.

33

The Glottal Stop

British English contains some sounds that are impossible to express with letters or combinations of letters. The reason is that these sounds are really *absences of sounds*, and the most ubiquitous and most frowned-upon of these is the glottal stop which might be described as 'strangling the "t" '.

For example, **what** becomes **wot** which then becomes **wo'**. Here's a sentence with four glottal stops:

Ber' finally go' sho' of 'is mo'uh

which, translated, means '**Bert finally got shot of his motor**'. Or, another example: ' **'E 'i' 'im**' which means '**He hit him**'. Come to think of it, how often nowadays do year hear the '**t**' sounded in **Gatwick**, or the two '**t**'s in **button**?

But the '**t**' isn't the only victim of the glottal (or **glo'al**) stop. The '**l**'s and '**ll**'s on the ends of words are becoming '**w**'s. **Bill** is pronounced something like **Beew**, **bull** becomes **boow**, and so on. No wonder the International Phonetic Alphabet indicates glottal stops with the **?** sign.

The glottal stop is spreading fast. Once the preserve of true Cockneys it migrated eastwards and is now a feature of what is known as Estuary English, the patois of a population that fans out from London to East Anglia in the north and to Kent in the south. And because our national speech has for centuries been influenced by what is spoken in and around London, so Estuary English is being disseminated and used throughout the land.

gefilte fish	geh-FIL-tuh fish
geisha	GAY-shuh
gendarme	ZHAHN-darm
germane	jer-MAYN
gestation	jes-TAY-shun
gesture	JES-choor
gesundheit	gez-OOND-tyt
geyser	GEE-zuh
ghetto	GET-toh
ghoul	gool
gibberish	JIB-ber-ish
gibbet	JIB-but
giblet	JIB-let
gigot	ZHEE-goh
gill	jill (*liquid measure*) gill (*fish*)
gimbals	JIM-buhls
glacé	GLAS-say
glisten	GLIS-suhn
gnat	nat
gnocchi	NYOK-kih
gnome	nohm
gnu	nyoo
government	GUV-ern-<u>ment</u> (*don't drop the first 'n'*)
goyim	GOY-yim
grievous	GREE-vus
grimace	grih-MAYSS
gunwale	GUN-nuhl
gymkhana	jim-KAR-nuh
gynaecologist	gy-nuh-KOL-uh-jist
gyrate	JY-rayt
gyroscope	JY-ruh-<u>scohp</u>
habitué	hah-BIT-u-ay
halcyon	HAL-sih-on
halfpenny	HAYP-nee
hallucinogen	hal-LOO-sin-uh-jen
handkerchief	HANG-kuh-<u>chif</u>
harangue	hah-RANG

35

harass	HAR-rus *is generally preferred to the more American* huh-RASS
harbinger	HAR-bin-jer
haricot	HAR-ih-coh
haute couture	oht-kuh-TYOOR
haute cuisine	oht-kwee-ZHEEN
hauteur	OH-ter

The Silent 'h'

Although somewhat blurred these days, the art of knowing when to sound (or aspirate) the **h** in words beginning with that letter is still important to many people. They know, for example, that the **'h'** is unaspirated in words like **heir, hour, honest** and **honour**, but aspirated in words like **hire, hole, homely** and **humour**.

They also know when to pronounce the **'h'** even when it is hidden in words like **wheel, white, while, what, which** and **why**; for these words the careful speaker and Scots in particular will blow out a positive **'hw'** sound: **hweel, hwite, hwile**, etc.

But joyous confusion reigns over the question of whether an **a** or an **an** precedes words beginning with **'h'**. Is it **a hotel**, or **an hotel**; **a hysterical person** or **an hysterical person**; **a historian** or **an historian**? And for that matter, is it **aitch**, or **haitch**?

---

hearsay	HEER-say
hearth	harth
hegemony	hih-GEM-uh-<u>nee</u> *or* HEJ-em-un-ee. *The American version is invariably* hej-EM-un-<u>ee</u>
heinous	HAY-nus

heir	ayr (*as in hair without the* '**h**')
haemorrhage	HEM-uh-<u>rij</u>
herb	herb ('erb *in the US*)
hiatus	hy-AY-tus
hiccough, hiccup	HIK-kup
hierarchy	HY-uh-rar-<u>kee</u>
hoi polloi	hoy-puh-LOY
homoeopathy	hoh-mih-OP-<u>path</u>-ee
homogeneous	<u>hoh</u>-muh-JEEN-yus, *meaning all the same, or uniform, is often confused with*
homogenous	hoh-MOJ-ih-<u>nus</u>, *meaning similar because of a common origin or ancestry. A further confusion arises with*
homogenise	hoh-MOJ-en-<u>eyes</u>, *meaning to make* **homogeneous,** *and which has nothing to do with its soundalike,* **homogenous.**

Of Homophones and Homonyms

A **homophone** is a word that is pronounced the same as another word but which is different in spelling, meaning and origin, like **boy** and **buoy**, **peace** and **piece**, **him** and **hymn**.

A **homonym** is a word that is spelt the same and sounds the same as another, but which has a different meaning, like **bank** (*savings bank, river bank, an aircraft turn*) and **bow** (*the bow of a ship, to bend over*). The word **bow** is also a homograph in that it has different pronunciations (*a knot, a weapon that shoots arrows, and a curve*). There are also homophonal phrases like **Isle of View/I love you**, and **having dinner at the old man's** and **having dinner at the Old Manse.**

honorarium	<u>on</u>-or-RAIR-ih-um
hors concours	or-koh(n)-koor
hors d'oeuvre	or-DERV
hospitable	HOS-pit-uh-buhl, *but* hos-PIT-uh-buhl *is also widely heard*
hover	HOV-ver
hubris	HYOO-bris
hyperbole	hy-PER-boh-lee
hyprocrite	HIP-uh-<u>krit</u>
hypocrisy	hih-POK-ruh-<u>see</u>

The International Phonetic Alphabet (IPA)

No European language possesses an alphabet that provides for all its sounds. The spoken English language, for example, is expressed in about forty different sounds but has only twenty-six letters to represent them. Sometimes combinations of letters are used to indicate sounds, like **sh** and **th**, but most of the time we have to remember that certain single letters can indicate different sounds, like 'c', which can be hard as in **crease**, or sibilant as in **cease**.

But there is an alphabet that does have a set of characters to indicate all the sounds of every language: the International Phonetic Alphabet. The IPA was constructed by phonologists over many years and while it uses many of the letters familiar to us they do not necessarily represent the equivalent sounds: 'j', for example, represents the sound of 'y' in English, and the diphthong œ represents the sound of 'a' as in **bad**. To cover all the sounds we use, the IPA includes some symbols strange to us, like ð for

iconoclast	eye-KON-oh-<u>klast</u>
idiosyncrasy	<u>id</u>-ee-oh-SING-kruh-see
idle	EYD-uhl
idol	EYE-dol
idyll	iddle (*to rhyme with* **piddle**) *but invariably* EY-dul *in the US*
ignominy	IG-nuh-min-ee
imbecile	IM-bih-seel *is preferred to* IM-bih-syl
impasse	ahm-<u>pas</u>
implacable	im-PLAK-uh-buhl
importune	<u>im</u>-poh-TYOON

the **th** sound, **3:** for the **er** sound, ʌ for the short '**u**' sound as in **bud** and **love**, ɔː for the **or** sound as in **brought** or **law**. A sentence in IPA looks a bit like Anglo-Saxon:

ð ə hɔːs dʒʌmpt ˈaʊva ðə fens

Whether you were British, German or Swedish, you would pronounce this sentence as:

The horse jumped over the fence

provided you knew your IPA or at least had a dictionary with IPA pronunciation, which virtually all dictionaries now have.

But as it would take at least an hour to learn the IPA symbols, this *One Hour Wordpower* book, intended after all for English users, merely asks you to observe only a few simple rules explained in the Pronunciation Guide on page 9.

Key to phonetic symbols for English

The International Phonetic Alphabet showing Received Pronunciation and General American Pronunciation

RP	Gen Am	Consonants	
•	•	p	pen, copy, happen
•	•	b	back, bubble, job
•	•	t	tea, tight, button
	•	t̬	city, better
•	•	d	day, ladder, odd
•	•	k	key, cock, school
•	•	g	get, giggle, ghost
•	•	tʃ	church, match, nature
•	•	dʒ	judge, age, soldier
•	•	f	fat, coffee, rough, physics
•	•	v	view, heavy, move
•	•	θ	thing, author, path
•	•	ð	this, other, smooth
•	•	s	soon, cease, sister
•	•	z	zero, zone, roses, buzz
•	•	ʃ	ship, sure, station
•	•	ʒ	pleasure, vision
•	•	h	hot, whole, behind
•	•	m	more, hammer, sum
•	•	n	nice, know, funny, sun
•	•	ŋ	ring, long, thanks, sung
•	•	l	light, valley, feel
•	•	r	right, sorry, arrange
•	•	j	yet, use, beauty
•	•	w	wet, one, when, queen

In foreign words only:

•	•	x	loch, chutzpah
•		ɬ	Llanelli, Hluhluwe

Vowels

- ɪ   kit, bid, hymn
- e   dress, bed
- æ   trap, bad
- ɒ   lot, odd, wash
- ʌ   strut, bud, love
- ʊ   foot, good, put

- iː   fleece, sea, machine
- eɪ   face, day, steak
- aɪ   price, high, try
- ɔɪ   choice, boy

- uː   goose, two, blue
- əʊ   goat, show, no
- oʊ   goat, show, no
- ɒʊ   *variant in* cold
- aʊ   mouth, now
- ɪə   near, here, serious
- eə   square, fair, various
- ɑː   start, father
- ɑː   lot, odd
- ɒː   thought, law
- ɔː   thought, law
- ɔː   north, war
- oː   *variant in* force, four
- ʊə   cure, poor, jury
- ɜː   nurse, stir
- ɝː   nurse, stir, courage

- i   happy, radiation, glorious

- ə   about, comma, common
- u   influence, situation, annual

- ɪ   intend, basic
- ʊ   stimulus, educate

In foreign words only:
- ɒ̃   grand prix, chanson
- ɑ̃ː   grand prix, chanson
- ɒ̃ː   chanson
- æ̃   vingt-et-un
- ɜ̃ː   vingt-et-un

impresario	<u>im</u>-pruh-SAR-ih-oh
imprimatur	<u>im</u>-prih-MAYT-uh
improvisation	im-<u>prov</u>-iz-AY-shun
impugn	im-PYOON
inadvertently	<u>in</u>-ad-VERT-unt-lee
inchoate	in-KOH-ayt
incomparable	in-COMP-ruh-<u>buhl</u>
inculcate	IN-kul-kayt
indefatigable	in-dih-FAT-ih-<u>guh-buhl</u>
indictment	in-DYT-munt
indisputable	<u>in</u>-dis-PYOO-tuh-buhl
inexorable	in-EKS-ruh-buhl
inexplicable	in-eks-PLIK-uh-buhl
infamous	IN-fah-mus
infinitesimal	<u>in</u>-fin-ih-TESS-ih-muhl
ingénue	AH(N)-zhah-nyoo
inhospitable	<u>in</u>-hos-PIT-ah-buhl *has largely replaced the former* in-HOS-pit-ah-buhl
inquiry, enquiry	in-KWY-uh-ree *or* in-KWY-ree. *The US pronunciation is invariably* IN-kwih-ree
insouciance	in-SOO-sih-ahnz
integral	IN-teh-gruhl
interlocutor	in-ter-LOK-yuh-ter
internecine	<u>in</u>-ter-NEE-syn
interstices	in-TER-<u>stuh</u>-sees
intestate	in-TESS-tayt
intestine	in-TESS-tin
intestinal	in-TESS-tin-ul
intravenous	in-truh-VEE-nus
invalid	IN-vuh-lid (*disabled*); in-VAL-lid (*not valid*)
inveigle	in-VAY-guhl
inventory	IN-vent-tree
irascible	ih-RAS-ih-buhl
irate	eye-RAYT
iron	EYE-un
irreparable	ih-REP-ruh-buhl

42

irrevocable	ih-REV-uh-kah-buhl
isosceles	eye-SOS-sih-lees
italic	ih-TAL-ik
itinerary	eye-TIN-er-uh-<u>ree</u>
jaguar	JAG-war (*to rhyme with jar*)
January	JAN-yoor-ee
jardinière	<u>zhar</u>-dih-NYAIR
jejune	zhi-ZHOON *or* jih-JOON
jeremiad	<u>jeh</u>-rih-MY-ad
jewellery	JOO-el-rih, *not* JOO-ler-ee
jocose	juh-KOHS
jocund	JOK-uhnd
joie de vivre	<u>zhwah</u>-duh-VEEV-ruh
junta	DJYOON-tuh; HOON-tuh *in the US*
kamikaze	<u>kam</u>-ih-KARZ-ee
kilometer	*logically, the pronunciation should be* KIL-uh-mee-tuh (SENT-ih-mee-tuh, MIL-ih-mee-tuh, etc.) *but* kil-OM-ih-tuh *is in common usage*
knish	kuh-NISH
knoll	noll
kosher	KOH-shuh
kudos	KYOO-dos
laboratory	lah-BOR-ah-<u>tree</u>
labyrinthine	<u>lab</u>-ah-RIN-thyn
lackadaisical	lak-uh-DAY-sih-<u>kuhl</u>
laconic	lak-ON-ik
laissez-faire	leh-say-FAIR
laity	LAY-ih-tih
lamentable	LAM-en-tuh-buhl
languor	LANG-ger
largess	lar-JESS
lascivious	luh-SIV-ih-<u>us</u>
laudatory	LOR-duh-<u>tree</u>

Verb and Noun Homographs

Many of our words are spelt the same but are pronounced differently (homographs), and they're waiting out there to trip us. The biggest group is of words which serve as both nouns and verbs: they look the same in each case but are stressed differently. Here are some to watch for:

WORD	NOUN PRONUN-CIATION	VERB PRONUN-CIATION
accent	AK-sent	ak-SENT
address	ad-RESS	ad-RESS
attribute	AT-rib-yoot	at-TRIB-yoot
combat	KOM-bat	kom-BAT
comment	KOM-ment	kom-MENT
compound	KOM-pound	kom-POUND
compress	KOM-press	kom-PRESS
conduct	KON-dukt	kon-DUKT
conflict	KON-flikt	kon-FLIKT
consort	KON-sort	kon-SORT
contest	KON-test	kon-TEST
contract	KON-trakt	kon-TRAKT
contrast	KON-trarst	kon-TRARST
convert	KON-vert	kon-VERT
convict	KON-vikt	kon-VIKT
defect	DEE-fekt	dih-FEKT
desert	DEZ-ert	dez-ERT

learned	LER-nud (*adjective*); lernd (*adverb*)
leitmotif	LYT-moh-<u>teef</u>
length	leng-th, *not* lenth
leprechaun	LEP-rih-korn
libido	lih-BEE-doh

44

detail	DE-tayl	dih-TAYL
digest	DY-jest	dih-JEST
discharge	DIS-charj	dis-CHARJ
discount	DIS-kount	dis-KOUNT
entrance	EN-trans	en-TRARNS
escort	ES-kort	es-KORT
exploit	EKS-ployt	eks-PLOYT
export	EKS-port	eks-PORT
extract	EKS-trakt	eks-TRACT
ferment	FER-ment	fer-MENT
import	IM-port	im-PORT
imprint	IM-print	im-PRINT
incense	IN-sens	in-SENS
increase	IN-krees	in-KREES
insult	IN-sult	in-SULT
object	OB-jekt	ob-JEKT
outlaw	OUT-lor	out-LOR
pervert	PER-vert	puh-VERT
present	PRES-ent	preh-ZENT
progress	PROH-gress	pruh-GRESS
project	PROH-jekt	proh-JEKT
rebel	REB-el	reh-BEL
refuse	REF-yoos	reh-FYOOS
second	SEK-und	sek-KOND
suspect	SUS-pekt	suh-SPEKT
survey	SER-vay	ser-VAY
transport	TRANS-port	trans-PORT
transfer	TRANS-fer	trans-FER

lichen	LY-kun
lien	LEE-en
lieu	lyoo
lieutenant	lef-TEN-unt; loo-TEN-unt *in the US*

lingerie	LAH(N)-zher-ee
liquorice	LIK-uh-riss
lithe	lyth
litigious	lih-TIJ-us
locale	loh-KARL
loch	lochhh
longevity	lon-JEV-ih-tee
louche	loosh
lubricious	loo-BRISH-us
lucre	LOO-ker
macabre	muh-KARB-ruh
Mach	
number	mahk number
machete	muh-SHET-ee
macho	MAT-choh
madam	MAD-dam
Madame	mah-DARM
Mademoiselle	mad-mwah-ZEL
maelstrom	MAYL-strom
maestro	MY-stroh
magazine	mag-ah-ZEEN (MAG-uh-zeen *in the US*)
magus	MAY-gus. *The plural is magi =* MAY-jy

Marry Merry Mary

In English, these three words are pronounced differently. In America, however, they are invariably pronounced the same: **MAIR-ree**. It was once a badge of good diction in New York where, in the well-heeled 'Butterfield' district of Manhattan (roughly between 60th and 96th Streets and Fifth and East End Avenues) you '*belonged*' if you could pronounce **Mary**, **marry** and **merry** so that they could be differentiated without further explanation.

maillot	mah-YOH
maitre d'hôtel	mey-truh-doh-TEL
malaise	mah-LAYZ
mandatory	MAN-dah-tree
maniacal	muh-NY-uh-kuhl
mannequin	MAN-ih-kin
maoeuvre	muh-NOO-vuh
mardi gras	mah-dih-GRAR
massage	MASS-arzh (mass-ARJ *in the US*)
matrix	MAY-triks
mauve	mohv
medicine	MED-ih-sin *is the usual style, but if you say* MED-sin *you will be deemed frightfully correct*
medieval	med-ih-EE-vul
mélange	muh-LARNZH
me–lée	MEH-lay
ménage à trois	muh-narzh-ah-trwar
meringue	muh-RANG
métier	may-teh-ay
midwifery	MID-wif-ree *or* mid-WIF-ree
mien	meen
migraine	MEE-grayn (MY-grayn *in the US*)
milieu	MEE-lyer
minute	MIN-nit (**time**); my-NYOOT (**tiny**)
minutiae	min-YOO-shee-ee
mirage	mih-RARZH
misanthrope	MIZ-an-thrope (*rhymes with* **hope**)
misanthropy	mih-ZAN-thro-pih
miscegenation	mis-ij-in-AY-shun
miscellany	mis-SEL-uh-nee
mischievous	MIS-chih-vus
misogynist	mih-SOJ-in-ist
misogyny	mih-SOJ-in-ee
missile	MISS-yl
mnemonic	nim-MON-ik
mocha	MOK-kuh

Don't be Mizzled

From the age of twelve the British poet Vernon Scannell was determined to be a writer. His education, throughout the 1920s and 1930s, had been patchy, but he was passionately fond of reading and was fascinated by words. But there was a snag, as he recollected in later years.

'I wasn't always sure how the words should really sound because my acquaintance with them had been made nearly always on the page and many of them I'd never actually heard spoken at all. We didn't possess what was then called a wireless until I was in my early teens and even when we did acquire one the only programmes I heard were news broadcasts, sports commentaries, or music hall comedians and singers. I was not only given no guide to pronunciation of my beloved words, I was positively misguided.

'My father, for instance, often used the word *mizzled* by which he meant deceived or led astray and when I came across the word *misled* on the printed page I instantly recognised it as *mizzled* and I pronounced it like that for some years before somebody put me right.'

moiré	MWAH-ray
momentarily	MOM-ment-trah-lee
momentary	MOH-men-tree
mongrel	MUNG-rel
Monsieur	meh-SYOOR
mores	MOR-ayz
mortgage	MOR-gidj
mousse	mooss
myxomatosis	mix-uh-muh-TOH-sis

nadir	NAY-deer
naiad	NY-ad
naïve	nahr-EEV *is the more correct, but* ny-EEV *is the more usual pronunciation*
naiveté	<u>nahr</u>-EEV-tay
nascent	NAYS-ent
nauseous	NOR-shus
née	nay
nephew	NEV-yoo *or* NEF-yoo
netsuke	NET-<u>soo</u>-kee
niche	*careful speakers use* nitch, *not* neesh
nihilism	NY-ih-lism
noblesse oblige	noh-BLES oh-BLEEZH
nomenclature	noh-MEN-kluh-<u>tyoor</u>
non sequitur	<u>non</u>-SEK-wit-uh
nouveau riche	<u>noo</u>-voh-REESH
nuance	NYOO-arns
nugatory	NYOO-guh-tree
obeisance	oh-BAY-sans
obese	oh-BEES
obfuscate	OB-fus-<u>kayt</u>
objet d'art	ob-zhay-DAR
obligatory	ob-LIG-uh-<u>tree</u>
obloquy	OB-luh-kwee
obstreperous	ob-STREP-uh-rus
occipital	ok-SIP-it-ul
occult	ok-KULT *or* OK-kult
oestrogen	EE-strud-jen
oeuvre	URV-ruh
often	offen
oligarchy	OL-ih-<u>gar</u>-kee
ombudsman	OM-boods-mun
omniscient	om-NIS-ih-ent
onerous	OHN-er-us
onyx	ON-niks
opprobrium	uh-PROH-brih-um
orgy	ORD-jee
origami	<u>or</u>-ih-GAR-mih

oriole	OR-rih-ohl
oscilloscope	os-SIL-uh-<u>skope</u>
osier	OH-zheer
otiose	OH-tih-yus *is the preferred pronunciation but this little-used word causes lots of confusion perhaps because* OH-shi-us *is the accepted American pronunciation. Use either, but be prepared to defend it!*
outré	OOH-tray
ouzo	OOH-zoh
oviparous	oh-VIP-ah-rus
pace (*Latin term*)	PAY-sih (*from the Latin* PAY-kih, *meaning 'with all deference to'*) *is common usage; also* PAY-chay
pachyderm	PAK-ih-<u>derm</u>
padrone	puh-DROH-nih
paean	PEE-ahn
paella	PY-el-uh
palais	PAL-lay
palaver	puh-LAR-vuh
palazzo	puh-LART-zoh
palfrey	PORL-free
panacea	<u>pan</u>-ah-SEE-uh
panache	puh-NASH
panegyric	<u>pan</u>-ih-JIH-rik (*to rhyme with* **lyric**)
paparazzi	<u>pah</u>-pah-RAT-zee; *the singular,* **paparazzo**, *is pronounced* <u>pah</u>-pah-RART-zoh
papier mâché	pap-yuh-MASH-ay
papillote	PAP-ih-loht
paprika	PAP-rih-kuh, *but also* puh-PREE-kuh
parabola	puh-RAB-uh-lah
paradigm	PAR-ah-<u>dym</u>
parenthesis	pah-REN-thuh-sis
pari-mutuel	<u>parry</u> <u>moo</u>-tyoo-ul
parochial	pah-ROH-kih-uhl

Perverse Pronunciation

Most of us are familiar with George Bernard Shaw's insistence that *ghoti* is pronounced **fish** ('**gh**' as in *rough*, '**o**' as in *women*, '**ti**' as in *motion*) to demonstrate the irrationality of English pronunciation. He might have also pointed out one example of '**gh**' being pronounced '**p**', as in *hiccough*. It seems, however, that GBS was unfamiliar with an 1882 American demonstration on the same theme, that **PHTHOLOGNYRRH** is actually pronounced **TURNER**, as follows:

> **PHTH** is pronounced like   **T**
> as in **PHTHISIC**
> **OLO** is pronounced like   **UR**
> as in **COLONEL**
> **GN** is pronounced like   **N**
> as in **GNAT**
> **YRRH** is pronounced like **ER**
> as in **MYRRH**

Of a later vintage is this contribution from a reader of *The Times*: 'Had the writer *sought* in his memory as he *ought*, *nought* would have prevented him from recalling that the *rough*-coated *dough*-faced *plough*man, as he strode *through* the streets of *Scarborough*, was *cough*ing and hic*cough*ing *thought*fully!'

Here's one to try yourself: see what common six-letter word you can make from **MNOMNOUPTE**. Allow yourself one minute. The answer is on page 95.

paroxysm	PAR-uk-siz-um
parquet	PARK-kay *is preferred to* PAR-kee
parterre	par-TEAR
partisan	par-tih-ZAN *seems to be gaining over its alternative,* PAR-tih-zahn
pas de deux	par-duh-<u>der</u>
passé	PAH-say
pastiche	pas-TEESH
pastille	pas-TEEL
pastrami	puh-STRAR-mih
pasty	PAS-tee (*to rhyme with* **mass**) *but there are regional variations, including* PARS-tee
patchouli	pah-CHOO-lih
pâté de foie gras	<u>pah</u>-tay-duh-fwar-grar
pathos	PAY-thos
patina	PAT-een-uh
patio	PAT-ih-oh, *not* PAY-shi-oh
pecan	PEE-kuhn
pecuniary	pih-KOO-nih-uh-<u>ree</u>
pedagogical	<u>ped</u>-ah-GOJ-ih-kul
pedagogue	PED-ah-<u>gog</u>
peignoir	payn-WAHR
pejorative	pih-JOR-uh-tiv
pellucid	peh-LYOO-sid
penchant	pah(n)-shah(n). *Not easy, this one, and probably a good one to avoid*
peon	PAY-on
père	pear
peremptory	puh-REMP-tuh-ree
pergola	PER-guh-luh
periphrasis	puh-IF-ruh-<u>sis</u>
peritoneum	per-ih-tuh-<u>NEE</u>-um
perorate	PER-uh-<u>rayt</u>
persiflage	PER-sih-flazh
persimmon	PER-sih-mun
personnel	<u>per</u>-suh-NEL
petard	pih-TARD

petite	pih-TEET
petits fours	peh-tih-FOOR
petits pois	peh-tih-PWAH
pharmacopoeia	far-muh-kuh-PEE-ah
phenyl	FEE-nyl *is preferred to* FEE-nil
philately	fih-LAT-ih-lee
phlegm	flem
phlegmatic	fleg-MAT-ik
phthisis	*The traditional pronunciation of* TY-sis *is giving way to* THY-sis
piano	pih-AN-oh (*the instrument*); pih-AR-noh (*the musical notation*)
pianoforte	pih-an-oh-FOR-tih
piazza	pih-ATZ-uh
picayune	pik-uh-YOON
picture	PIK-tyoor
pied-à-terre	pyay-duh-TAIR
pince-nez	PAH(N)S-nay
piquant	PEE-kahnt
pique	peek
pissoir	PEE-swar
piste	peest
pituitary	pih-TYOO-it-ree
pizza	PEET-zah
placate	pluh-KAYT
placatory	PLAK-at-uh-ree *or* plah-KAY-tuh-ree
placebo	plah-SEE-boh
plagiarism	PLAY-ji-ah-rism
plaid	plad
plait	plat
plaque	plark
plat du jour	PLAH-dur-zhoor
pleasance	PLEZ-enz
plebeian	plih-BEE-yun
plebiscite	PLEB-ih-sit
plethora	PLETH-uh-ruh
podiatry	poh-DEE-uh-tree *appears to have an edge on* poh-DY-uh-tree

Pronunciation Maps

How do you pronounce the word **chimney**? **CHIM-nee**? **CHIM-lee**? **CHIM-blee**? It's all of these, and more, depending upon where you live in Britain. There still remain among us pockets of dialect speakers who, despite the standards of Received Pronunciation (more on that later) will insist that their particular way of saying a word is the correct one, and to hell with the rest.

Between 1948 and 1961 the Universities of Leeds and Sheffield surveyed dialects in 300 locations throughout England, and a series of 'pronunciation' or 'word' maps was the result. This atlas of dialects shows that while further (to express distance) is pronounced **FER-ther** in half the country, the other half will say **FAR-ther**. And while a flea is a **flea** in the South, it is a **flen** in Shropshire, a **lop** in Yorkshire and a **fleck** in Lancashire.

Courtesy of WORD MAPS:
A Dialect Atlas of England.
Clive Upton, Stewart Sandevson
and John Widdowson
Routledge Publishers, 1987.

poignant	POYN-yant
polemic	puh-LEM-ik
poltergeist	POL-tuh-gyst
polysyllabic	pol-ih-sih-LAB-ik
pomegranate	*The quaint traditional pronunciation,* POM-gran-it, *is now completely replaced by* POM-ih-gran-it
porcelain	PORS-lin *or* PORS-ih-lin
portentous	por-TEN-tus, *not* por-TEN-shus

54

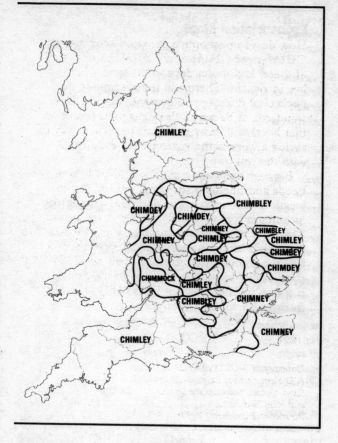

portmanteau	port-MAN-toh
poseur	poh-ZER
posse	POSS-ee
posthumous	POS-tyoo-mus
pot-pourri	poh-pooh-REE
prebendary	PREB-end-ree
precedence	PRES-ih-dens
precinct	PREE-singt
preciosity	presh-ih-OS-it-ee

premise	PREM-iss
presage	PRESS-ij
present	PREZ-ent (*noun*); preh-ZENT (*verb*)
pretence	prih-TENS
prima donna	PREE-muh DON-uh
prima facie	PRY-muh FAY-shee
primarily	PRY-mar-ih-lee
privacy	PRIV-uh-see
private	PRY-vat
privy	PRIV-ee
prix fixe	pree feeks
proboscis	proh-BOSS-is
process	PROH-sess (*noun*); proh-SESS (*verb*)
promissory	PROM-iss-uh-ree
propinquity	pruh-PING-kwih-tee
propitious	pruh-PISH-us
pro rata	proh-RAH-tuh
prosaic	proh-ZAY-ik
prosciutto	proh-SHOOT-oh
proselytise	PROS-eh-lit-<u>eyes</u>
protégé	PROT-eh-zhay
proviso	pruh-VY-zoh
pseudonym	SYOO-duh-nim
psittacosis	sit-uh-KOH-sis
psyche	SY-kee
psychosis	sy-KOH-sis
ptarmigan	TAR-mih-gun
ptomaine	tuh-MAYN
puerile	PYOO-uh-ryl
puisne	PYOO-nih
puissance	PYOO-ih-zuhns, *or* PWIH-sahns, *which is closer to the French pronunciation*
pulchritude	PUL-krih-<u>chood</u>
pumice	PUM-iss
punitive	PYOO-nih-tiv
purlieu	PER-lyoo

purport	puh-PORT
pursuivant	PER-sih-<u>vunt</u>
pusillanimous	<u>pyoo</u>-sih-LAN-ih-mus
pustule	PUS-tyool
putative	PYOO-tuh-tiv
putrescent	pyoo-TRES-sent
pyramidal	pih-RAM-ih-duhl
Pyrrhic	PIH-rik
quaff	kwoff
qualm	kwarm
quandary	KWON-duh-ree
quantum	KWON-tum
quark	kwark
quasar	KWAY-zar
quash	kwosh
quasi-	KWAYZ-eye-
quay	kee
quenelle	keh-NEL

The Pterrible Ptarmigan

The English language still hangs on to a few
words that retain the Greek habit of prefixing
words beginning with the sounds 's' and 't' with
a 'p'. When we pronounce them we ignore the 'p'
entirely: **psychology, psychedelic,
pseudonym, psittacosis, psoriasis;
ptomaine; pterodactyl** and, of course, that
curious grouse, the **ptarmigan**:

> The ptarmigan is pterrible,
> As ill-ptempered as can be.
> He ptarries not on ptelephone poles,
> Nor ptwitters from a ptree.
> And the way he ptakes pto spelling
> Is a ptiresome pthing pto me.

queue	kyoo
quiche	keesh
quiescent	kwee-ESS-unt
quietus	kwy-EE-tus
quinine	kwih-NEEN
quintessence	kwin-TES-sens

Quotations

'I once worked with a Chinese fellow in England who when things went wrong would mutter darkly, "Bruddy hairo!" which I took to be some ancient Chinese invective; it was not until many months later that I realized he was just saying, "Bloody hell!" ' – *American writer Bill Bryson, 1990*

'If anyone corrects your pronunciation of a word in a public place, you have every right to punch him in the nose.' – *American columnist Heywood Broun*

'What I tried to get was a style or quality of English which would not be laughed at in any part of the country.' – *Lord Reith, former Director-General of the BBC, 1957*

'. . . even here in London, they clip their words after one manner about the Court, another in the City, and a third in the suburbs . . .' – *Jonathan Swift, 1712*

'They spell it Vinci and pronounce it Vinchy; foreigners always spell better than they pronounce.' – *Mark Twain*

'I wanted them to change it to tart. Scrubber implies someone who can't talk properly, and wears horrible clothes, but I always spoke well, and had good clothes . . .' – *former call-girl Christine Keeler, objecting to being described as a 'scrubber'.*

quixotic	kwik-SOT-tik
quorum	KWOR-ruhm
quotidian	kwoh-TID-ih-un
rabbi	RAB-by
rabid	RAB-id (*but rabies* = RAY-bees)
raconteur	rak-on-TUHR
radii	RAY-dih-eye
ragout	rah-GOO
raison d'être	ray-zoh(n) det-ruh
rampage	RAM-pij (*noun*); ram-PAYJ (*verb*)
rancour	RAN-kur
rapport	rah-POOR
rapprochement	rap-PROSH-moh(n)
ratatouille	rat-ah-TWEE
ratio	RAY-shoh
ratiocination	rat-ih-OS-ih-nay-shun
raucous	ROR-kus
really	reer-uh-lee (*as in* clearly)
recalcitrant	ree-KAL-si-trant
receipt	rih-SEET
réchauffé	ray-showf-ay
recherché	rah-SHAIR-shay
recidivist	reh-SID-ih-vist
recipe	RES-ih-pee
recognizance	reh-KOG-nih-zanz
recognise	REK-og-nyz (*not* rekernize)
recondite	REK-on-dyt
reconnaissance	rih-KON-ih-sans
reggae	REGG-ay
regime	ray-ZHEEM
remedial	reh-MEE-dih-al
remonstrate	REM-on-strayt
Renaissance	ruh-NAY-sahns
rendezvous	RON-dih-voo
renege	reh-NAYG *and* reh-NEEG *are about equal in popularity*
repartee	rep-uh-TEE
repertoire	rep-uh-TWAHR
reportage	rep-uh-TARZH

Received Pronunciation (RP)

The sounds of English have come a long way:
from the ancient Britons via the Romans,
Anglo-Saxons, Normans and, latterly,
Americans. British speech in the Middle Ages
was a hodgepodge of dialects until, with the
invention of printing and the establishment of
learning centres, a process of standardisation
began. Spellings changed, vowels shifted, and
along with hundreds of other words, a **hoos** in
Chaucer's time became a **hoss** in Shakespeare's
day and a **house** by the nineteenth century.
London, as the country's centre of commerce,
the Church and the Court, and Oxford and
Cambridge, as its chief centres of learning, were
at the forefront of these changes and thus the
most standardised. The further you travelled
from these centres, the more marked speech
differences would be.

The emergence and development of the public
school system in the mid-nineteeth century
completed the job of standardisation; students
simply had their local accents knocked out of
them. And, noting the formula of right school/

requiescat	<u>rek</u>-wih-ES-kat
reprise	ruh-PREES
reredos	REER-dohs
research	rih-SERTCH (REE-sertch *in the US*)
rescind	rih-SIND
resin, rosin	rezzin
respite	RES-pit (*the older* RES-pyt *is falling out of use*)
resume	reh-ZYOOM
résumé	REH-zyoo-may

proper accent = automatic entry into society, top jobs, clubs and families, grammar schools soon followed. It was an elitist kind of standardisation, of course, and became known as PSP – Public School Pronunciation.

Disseminated by the schools, universities, the clergy and – from the 1920s – by the BBC, Public School Pronunciation, now known as RP, was soon widely recognised as the correct way to speak even though it was hardly relevant to the majority of the population.

But over the past couple of decades there has been a decided swing away from RP as a preferred accent, and its defenders have seen regional accents park their Sierras and Cavaliers on their carefully tended lawns. Now a bus has arrived, spilling out Estuary English. Perhaps these latest loud arrivals, unconscious pioneers of a new Standard English that isn't exactly music to many ears, will help rather than destroy the cause of RP as the most desired style of speech in Britain.

retina	RET-ih-nah
retinue	RET-ih-nyoo
retroussé	reh-TROO-say
reveille	rih-VAL-ee
ribald	RIH-buhld
riband	RIH-bund
ricochet	RIK-oh-shay
riposte	rih-POST (*to rhyme with* **lost**)
risible	RIS-ih-buhl (*as in* **visible**)
risqué	RIS-kay
robust	roh-BUST

roué	ROO-ay
rout	rowt (*to rhyme with* **out**)
route	root (*as in* **boot**; rowt *in the US*)
routier	ROOT-yay
rowlocks	ROL-loks
rutabaga	<u>roo</u>-tuh-BAY-guh
saboteur	<u>sab</u>-uh-TER
saccharin	(*the compound*) SAK-uh-rin
saccharine	(*the adjective*) SAK-ar-<u>eyn</u> *is generally preferred to* SAK-ar-<u>een</u>
sacerdotal	<u>sass</u>-uh-DOH-tuhl
sacrilegious	sak-rih-LIJ-us
sagacity	suh-GAS-ih-tee
sake	(*the Japanese drink*) SAY-kih
salade niçoise	sal-<u>lud</u>-nih-SWARZH
saline	SAY-lyn
salon	SAH-loh(n)
saloon	suh-LOON
salsify	SAL-sih-fee
salutary	SAL-yuh-tree
sang-froid	sah(n)-frwah
sangria	san-GREE-uh
sanguine	SANG-gwin
satiate	SAY-shih-ayt
saturnine	SAT-uh-<u>nyn</u>
satyr	SAT-eh
sauté	soh-tay
savant	SAV-uhnt (sah-VARNT *in the US*)
savoir-faire	sav-wahr-FAIR
scallop	SKOL-lup
Schadenfreude	SHAR-dehn-<u>froy</u>-duh
schedule	SHED-yool (SKED-yool *in the US*)
scherzo	SKERT-zoh
schism	SKIZ-um (*Longman states that the SIZ-um pronunciation is preferred by only 29% of its speaker's panel*)
schizoid	SKIT-soyd
schizophrenia	skit-soh-FREE-nih-uh

62

schlemiel	shleh-MEEL
sciatica	sy-AT-ik-uh
scimitar	SIM-ih-tuh
scintilla	sin-TIL-luh
scintillate	SIN-til-ayt
scion	sy-un
scone	skone (*to rhyme with* **bone**) *although there are regional variations like* skon

The Schwa

Say the word **minus**, naturally, and listen to what comes out. It isn't exactly **my-nuss**; more like **my-noos** or **my-n's**; in fact, to a foreign ear the '**u**' would be hard to detect at all. What we are expressing here is an unstressed, unaccented vowel. Try another word: **variety**. We do not enunciate **vah-ry-eh-tee**, do we? It comes out, naturally, is **vry-uh-tih**. So what's happened to the '**a**' and the '**e**'?

What has happened is that these vowels have been neutralised, and a large proportion of our words are pronounced with neutral vowels – so neutral that all five vowels sound about the same. To indicate neutral vowels, phoneticians use a little typographical device called a *schwa* (ə), so that in a dictionary using the International Phonetic Alphabet, the words above would appear as:

minus ˈmaɪnəs   *variety* vəˈraɪəi

In *Say it Right*, we have, as explained in the **Pronunciation Guide**, dispensed with all such symbols in favour of instantly recognisable syllables.

63

scourge	skurj (*to rhyme with* **urge**)
scrod	(*the fish*) skrod, *but sometimes* skrood, *an echo of the original Old Dutch* **schrode**, *and later Dutch* **schrood**
scythe	syth (*th as in* **father**)
seance	SAY-ahns
sebaceous	sih-BAY-shus
secretary	SEK-reh-<u>tree</u>
segue	SEG-way
seismic	SYZ-mik
senescent	sen-ESS-unt
senile	SEE-nyl
senility	sih-NIL-ih-tee
sentient	SEN-shee-unt
sepulchre	SEP-ul-kuh
sequester	sih-KWES-ter
serendipity	<u>ser</u>-en-DIP-ih-tee
serum	SEE-rum
sesame	SES-ih-mee
sewage	SOO-ij
sewerage	SOO-er-ij
sheikh	shayk
shibboleth	SHIB-uh-<u>leth</u>
signor, signora	SEE-nyor; see-NYOR-uh
shillelagh	shih-LAY-lee
silhouette	<u>sil</u>-ooh-ET
simile	SIM-ih-lee
simulacrum	<u>sim</u>-yuh-LAY-krum
sinecure	SIN-ih-kyoor
sinistral	SIN-is-truhl
slalom	SLAR-lom
sloth	slohth
slough	(*cast skin*) sluff; (*swamp or bog*) slow, *to rhyme with* **cow**
sluice	sloos
sobriquet	SOH-brih-<u>kay</u>
soi-disant	<u>swah-de-zah(n)</u>
soigné, soignée	<u>SWAH</u>-nyay

64

Silent Letters

The American wordsmith Richard Lederer came up with an ingenious list of twenty-six words in which in each word a letter of the alphabet is silent when pronounced:

A. bread **B.** doubt **C.** indict
D. handkerchief **E.** height **F.** halfpenny **G.** gnome **H.** rhyme **I.** bait **J.** rijsttafel (*yes, it exists; look it up*) **K.** know **L.** would
M. mnemonic **N.** column **O.** people
P. pneumonia **Q.** racquet **R.** forecastle
S. aisle **T.** rapport **U.** gauge **V.** savvy
W. answer **X.** Grand Prix **Y.** crayon
Z. rendezvous

Lederer admits that he's plainly cheating with **savvy** (the second 'v' is silent, sort of), and is stretching things a bit far with **rijsttafel**. Any suggestions for substitutions?

soirée	SWAH-ray
sojourn	soh-JERN
solace	SOL-lis
solder	SORL-duh (SORD-ar *in the US*)
solecism	SOL-ih-sizum
sommelier	som-UHL-yay
sonorous	SON-er-us
sotto voce	sot-toh-VOH-chay
soufflé	SOO-flay
sough	(*sighing wind*) sow, *to rhyme with* cow; (*drain*) suff
soupçon	SOOP-soh(n)
species	SPEE-sheez
sphincter	SFING-tuh
sphinx	sfingks

spiel	shpeel
spontaneity	spon-tuh-NY-et-ee
staccato	stuh-KAR-toh
stalwart	STORL-wut
starboard	STAR-bud
status	STAY-tus
stanch	starnch
staunch	stornch (*both* **stanch** *and* **staunch** *have the same meaning*)
sterile	STEH-ryl

Strine and Fraffly

Pronunciation and accents are always good for a laugh. Take Strine, an extreme, nasalised dialect of Australian English in which *bison* = basin, *egg nisher* = air conditioner, *egg jelly* = actually and, indeed, *Strine* = Australian. '*Zarf trawl, we rony fleshun blud wennit saul boil down*' and '*Y'can have yur baked necks in garbler mince*' translates as 'After all, we're only flesh and blood when it's all boiled down', and 'You can have your bacon and eggs in a couple of minutes', respectively.

Strine was the discovery or invention of Afferbeck Lauder (alphabetical order), the pseudonym of Australian author Alistair Morrison who unleashed it on to an unsuspecting world in 1962.

But the toffee-nosed, frightfully-English dialect did not escape Lauder's attention either. Identified as Fraffly, this dialect is not always easy to crack, especially with such terms as *egg-wetter gree* ('Yes, I quite agree with you'); *Rich In Spock* (I saw her in Regent's Park); *common simian* ('Do come and see me in a day or so'), not to mention names like *Tawneh, Undraw, Hillrair* and *Vellrair*.

stevedore	STEE-vuh-dor
stigmata	stig-MAH-tuh
stipend	STY-pund
stipendiary	sty-PEN-dih-ar-ee
stoic	STOH-ik
strength	*Sound the* **'g'**; *it is not* strenth!
strychnine	STRIK-nin
suave	swarv
subpoena	sub-PEE-nuh
subsidence	sub-SY-dunts, *but there is about equal preference for* SUB-sih-dunts
succinct	SUK-sinkt
suede	swayd
suffice	suh-FYSS (*to rhyme with* ice)
suite	sweet
supine	SOOP-eyn
surmise	ser-MYZ
surveillance	ser-VAY-lans
survey	ser-VAY (*verb*); SER-vay (*noun*)
svelte	svelt or sfelt
sycophant	SIK-uh-fant
sycophantic	sik-uh-FAN-tik
syllogism	SIL-uh-jiz-um
symbiosis	SIM-bih-oh-sis
synergy	SIN-er-jee
synod	SIN-ud
tableau	TAB-loh
table d'hôte	TAR-bluh doht
tacit	TAS-sit
taco	TAR-koh
tagliatelli	tal-yuh-TEL-lih
taipan	TY-pan
tarot	TAH-roh
tartare (*sauce*)	tahr-tahr
tempera	TEM-pruh
temporarily	TEMP-ruh-ril-ee
tempura	tem-PYOO-ruh
tenet	TEN-net

tensile	TEN-syl
tenure	TEN-yoor; *alternatively,* TEN-yuh
tequila	teh-KEE-luh
terrazzo	teh-RAHT-soh
tertiary	TER-shih-ree
tête-à-tête	tayt-uh-TAYT
tiara	tee-AR-ruh
timbre	*Difficult enough in French,* tah(n)-bruh, *but acceptable English approximations are* TAMB-ruh *and* TIMB-ruh
timpani	TIM-puh-nee
tirade	ty-RAYD
titular	TIT-yoo-luh
toccata	tok-KAR-tuh
tonne	tun

Top Pipple's Spich

The 'Fraffly' dialect of English isn't entirely a joke, for there is a teeth-grinding extension of RP that comes close to it. Among its affectations are:

Substitute E for A	**seddle, rebble, relly, repture, rettle**
Substituting I for OU	**grise** for grouse, **hise** for house
Substituting OR for O	**orf, clorth, orften, frorth, lorst**
Substituting IH for Y	**short-lih, similar-lih, shocking-lih**

And, *especial-lih*, dropping the 'g' from many words like **huntin'**, **shootin'** and **fishin'** while at the same time *emphasisin'* the final syllable: **hun-TIN, shoo-TIN, fish-IN.**

toque	tohk
torque	tork
tortilla	tor-TEE-yuh
toucan	TOO-kahn
touché	TOO-shay
toupee	too-PAY
tourniquet	TOOR-nih-<u>kay</u>
trait	trayt
tranche	trarnsh
traverse	TRAV-ers (*noun*); trah-VERS (*verb*)
trepan	trih-PAN
tribunal	try-BYOO-nul
tribune	TRIB-yoon
tricot	TREE-koh
tripartite	<u>try</u>-PAR-tyt
tripos	TRY-pos
triptych	TRIP-tik
triumvirate	try-UM-vrit
troth	trohth (*to rhyme with* **growth**)
tsetse fly	TZET-see
tulle	tyool
turquoise	TER-kwoyz
tutti-frutti	TOO-tih FROO-tih
twelfth	*pronounce as spelt*: twel-f-th
twopenny, twopence	TUP-pun-ee, TUP-punts
ukelele	<u>yoo</u>-kyoo-LAY-lee
ululation	yool-yoo-LAY-shun
umbilical	um-BIL-ih-kal
umbrage	UM-brij
umbrella	um-BREL-luyh (*not* um-ber-ell-ah)
umlaut	OOM-lowt
unanimity	<u>yoo</u>-nuh-NIM-it-ee
unctuous	UNG-choo-us
unguent	UNG-wunt
urethra	yoo-REE-thruh
urinal	YOO-ri-nuhl *or* yoo-RY-nuhl
urine	YOOR-in

69

In Search of the Unpronounceable

Wales may be next door to England, but to most English eyes and ears its language could belong to a race on another planet. Without a guide, words like **cwpwrda** (cupboard), **cwrw** (beer), **ffwrdd** (away), **tlws** (pretty) and **wfft** (blow) appear to be bafflingly unpronounceable, although they flow from Welsh tongues with enviable ease.

Naturally, we look upon our own language as a model of logic. But what are non-English speakers (or even English speakers!) to make of such consonantal combinations as **sthm**, **tchphr** and **tchst**?

Curiously enough we use them almost every day – in such words as **asthmatic**, **catchphrase** and **matchstick**.

usual	*Careful speakers retain the two 'u's:* YOOS-you-uhl
usurious	yoo-ZHOOR-ih-us
usury	YOOS-ree
usurp	yoo-ZERP
uxorious	uks-OR-ih-us
vaccinate	VAK-sin-ayt
vaccine	VAK-seen
vacillation	vas-sil-AY-shun
vagina	vuh-JY-nah
vaginal	vuh-JY-nuhl
valance	VAL-lants
valet	*Those rich enough to afford one call him a* VAL-lit; *for the rest of us the usual pronunciation is* VAL-ay
valise	vah-LEES
vase	varz

70

vegetable	VEJ-tuh-buhl
vehement	VEE-eh-ment
vehicular	vee-HIK-yoo-luh
veld	feldt
velour	vel-OOR
verbatim	ver-BAY-tim
verdure	VERD-juh
verisimilitude	<u>ver</u>-ih-sih-MIL-ih-tyood
verité	vay-reh-TAY
verruca	veh-ROO-kuh
vertiginous	ver-TIJ-in-us
veterinary	VET-rin-ree
vicarious	vih-KAIR-ih-us (*to rhyme with* **hair**)
vichyssoise	vee-shih-SWAHZ
vicissitude	vih-SIS-ih-<u>tyood</u>
victualler	VIT-el-uh
victuals	VIT-ulz
vide	VY-dih
vigneron	VEE-nyer-or(n)
vignette	vin-YET
vilify	VIL-ih-fy
villain	VIL-lin
viola	Take your choice from vih-OH-luh *and* vy-OH-luh (*the instrument*); *and* VY-oh-lah *and* vy-OH-lah (*the flower*)
virago	vih-RAR-goh
virulent	VIH-roo-lunt
visage	VIS-ij
vis-à-vis	veez-uh-vee
visceral	VISS-er-al
viscid	VIS-sid
viscount	VY-kount
vitamin	VIT-uh-min (VY-tah-min *in US*)
vitiate	VISH-ih-ayt
vituperation	vy-tyoo-puh-RAY-shun
voile	voy-il
vol-au-vent	vol-ah-voh(n)

Vine Talk

With the great growth of wine drinking, more and more people are keen to know how to read from a label without the embarrassing pause, stumble or hiccup. Here are some fairly common names and terms associated with wine that can cause momentary panic. Keep in mind that some of those listed here have regional variations but nevertheless they should keep you ahead of the average wine merchant.

Aligote	ah-lih-goh-TAY
Alsace	al-SASS
Amontillado	ah-mon-tih-YAR-doh
Anjou	AWN-zhoo
appellation	ah-pel-AH-syah(n)
d'origine	DOR-rih-jeen
Beaujolais	BOH-zhoh-lay
blanc de blancs	blaw(n)-duh-blaw(n)
Brouilly	*BREW-yih*
brut	broot
Cahors	kar-OR
Cassis	kah-SEES
Chablis	shab-LEE
Chateauneuf-du-pape	sho-tuh-nuff-duh-parp
Chenin blanc	SHAY-nan blaw(n)
Cinsault	san-soh
Corbieres	cor-bih-AYR (*to rhyme with* **hair**)
Dom Perignon	dorm PAY-rih-NYORN

72

Entre-Deux-Mers	<u>awn</u>-truh-duh-<u>mair</u>
Graves	grarv
Liebfraumilch	LEEB-fruh-milsh
Loire	luh-wahr
Maçon	MAK-orn
Malaga	MAL-ah-gah
Mercurey	MAIR-koo-ray
Merlot	MAIR-loh
Meursault	MEER-soh
Minervois	me-nair-<u>vwah</u>
Montrachet	<u>morn</u>-rah-SHAY
mousseux	moo-SER
Muscadet	MOOS-kuh-day
Niersteiner	NEER-shty-ner
Nuits-Saint-Georges	nwee-sahn-zhorz
Pouilly Fuissé	POO-yee FWEE-say
Pouilly Fumé	POO-yee FYOO-may
Riesling	REES-ling
Rioja	ree-oh-kuh
rosé	roh-ZAY
Sancerre	SORN-sair
Sauterne	SOH-tairn
Sauvignon	SOH-veen-yorn
Souve	SWAH-vay
Spätlese	SHPAYT-lay-zuh
Sur Lie	SOOR-lee
Vinho verde	VEEN-ho vair-day
vin ordinaire	vah(n) or-dih-NAIHR

vouchsafe	<u>vowtch</u>-SAYF
voyeur	vwah-YOOR

Try the WQXR Test

WQXR is a New York classical music radio
station whose announcers pride themselves on
correct and elegant diction. All prospective
announcers are given the following test which
must be read pronunciation-perfect before an
application is even considered:

'The old man with the flaccid face and dour
expression grimaced when asked if he were
conversant with zoology, mineralogy, or the
culinary arts. "Not to be secretive," he said, "I
may tell you that I'd given precedence to the
study of genealogy. But, since my father's
demise, it has been my vagary to remain
incognito because of an inexplicable, lamentable,
and irreparable schism. It resulted from a
heinous crime, committed at our domicile by
an impious scoundrel. To err is human . . . but
this affair was so grievous that only my inherent
acumen and consummate tact saved me." '

---

wagon-lit	vag-ar(n)-lee
waistcoat	WESS-kit *is the traditional pronunciation but today it is generally* WAYST-koht
walnut	WORL-nut (*not* WAR-nut)
werewolf	WEER-woolf
wizened	WIZZ-end
worsted	WOOS-ted
wort	wert
wrath	roth

wildebeest	VILD-uh-<u>beest</u>
wunderkind	VOON-duh-kint
xenophobia	<u>zen</u>-uh-FOH-bih-ah
xerography	zih-ROG-rah-<u>fee</u>
xylophone	ZY-luh-<u>fohn</u>

Youth on Accents

In 1970, 177 South Wales and Somerset school children were quizzed on their attitudes to various British accents and the social status associated with them. Here's the league table according to the kids:

1 Received Pronunciation	5 Northern English
2 'Affected' RP	6 Somerset
3 South Welsh	7 Cockney
4 Irish	8 Birmingham

---

yarmulka	YAR-muhl-kuh
yashmak	YASH-mak
yoghurt	YOHG-uht
zabaglione	zah-barl-YOH-nee
zealot	ZEL-uht
Zeitgeist	TZYT-gyst
zouave	zoo-ARV

Are You Saying It Right

Here are a few quick quizzes to test your pronunciation skills. You'll find the answers on pages 95–6.

Make a Choice

1 **longevity**   lon-GEV-ih-tee *or* lon-JEV-ih-tee
2 **extempore**   ek-stem-POOR *or* ik-STEM-pree
3 **mohican**   moh-HEE-kun *or* MOH-ih-kahn
4 **kibitz**   kih-BITS *or* KIB-bits
5 **odium**   OH-jum *or* OH-dyum

A Spell at Games

Here are the names of some common-enough games. How do you pronounce them?

baccarat	backgammon	bezique
boule	chemin de fer	croquet
euchre	jai alai	piquet
	vingt-et-un	

Medical Matters

These days it's difficult to avoid being drawn into discussions on illnesses and treatments. Trouble is, many medical terms are a challenge to pronounce correctly. How would you fare with the following fairly common terms?

collagen	endocrine	endoscopy
Eustachian tube	gingivitis	histamine
intravenous	*in vitro*	laparoscopy
occipital lobe	peristalsis	placebo

Occupations

Now try these occupations and professions:

1	**anaesthetist**	an-EESS-thuh-tist *or* an-es-THEE-tist
2	**antiquary**	an-TIH-kwah-ree *or* AN-tik-war-ree
3	**artificer**	ART-if-is-er *or* ar-TIF-is-er
4	**chauffeur**	shoh-FER *or* SHOH-fuh
5	**comptroller**	kon-TROLL-er *or* KOMP-trol-luh
6	**gynaecologist**	jy-nuh-KOL-uh-jist *or* gy-nuh-KOL-uh-jist
7	**orthopaedist**	orth-OP-ih-dist *or* orth-oh-PEE-dist
8	**sommelier**	SOM-ih-leer *or* som-UHL-yay

Music to the Ear

Finally, can you strike the correct note with these terms?

antiphony	**arpeggio**	**barcarole**	*étude*
improvisation	**pizzicato**	**tutti**	**vibrato**

British Place-names

The place-names of Britain form a national network of verbal trip-wires with their archaic, dialectal and often hopelessly daft pronunciations.

The quaintness of English place-name pronunciation is well recognised, but journey into Scotland where Gaelic (or Erse) still lurks, and you face real challenges. The poet A. D. Hope, upon learning that Cuchullin (formerly Cuchulain) Hills was pronounced KOO-lin, promptly wrote:

The pronunciation of Erse
Gets worse and worse:
They spell it Cuchulain –
No fuchulain.

Here is a selection of the more vexing English, Irish
and Scottish place-names, occasionally with their
archaic or local dialect forms. Note that Welsh place-
names are listed separately.

Alcester	UHL-stuh *or* ORL-stuh
Aldeburgh	ORL-bruh *or* ORL-buh-ruh
Alnwick	AN-nik
Altrincham	ORL-tring-um
Armagh	ahr-MAR
Arundel	AHR-un-duhl
Auchmuty	ok-MYUT-ih
Auchtermuchty	ok-tuh-MUK-tih
Balquhidder	BAL-wid-deer
Beauchamp Place	BEE-cham
Beaulieu	BYOO-lih
Beauvoir	BOH-vwar
Belvoir Castle	BEE-vuh
Berkeley	BARK-lih
Berkshire	BARK-sheer
Berwick	BEH-rik
Beswick	BEZ-zik
Bicester	BIS-ter
Borrowstouness	*The traditional pronunciation is, rather quaintly,* BOH-nes
Buccleuch	buk-LOO
Buittle	BIT-tuhl, *but sometimes* BYOO-tuhl
Bury	BEH-rih
Cadogan Place	kah-DUG-un
Calke (Derby)	kork, *but sometimes* kuk
Calne (Wilts)	karn
Cerne Abbas	<u>sern</u> AB-bus

Cheyne Walk	SHAY-nih
Chiswick	CHIZ-zik
Cinque Ports	singk ports
Cirencester	SY-run-<u>ses</u>-tuh *has now overwhelmed the traditional form of SIS-eh-ter*
Cliveden	KLIV-den
Clovelly	kluh-VEL-lih
Colne	kohn (*to rhyme with* **Rome**)
Crossmaglen	KROS-muh-glen
Dalziel (S. Clyde)	dee-ELL
Dumbarton	dum-BAR-tun
Dungeness	<u>dun</u>-juh-NESS
Eigg	egg
Eynsham	EN-shum
Eythorne	AY-thun
Fenwick	FEN-ik
Feock	FEE-ok
Feoffees	FEE-fees
Fermanagh	feh-MAN-nuh
Fowey	foy
Glamorgan	glah-MOR-gun
Goudhurst	GOWD-herst (*to rhyme with* **crowd**)
Great Hautbois	grayt-HOB-bis
Greenock	GRIH-nuk
Greenwich	GREN-idj, *though often* GREN-itch
Hardres	hardz
Harwich	HAR-idj
Hertford	HART-fud
Hertfordshire	HART-fud-<u>sheer</u>
Hoxne (Suffolk)	HOK-sun

Ibrox Park	EYE-broks
Ide (Devon)	id, *but often* eed
Ightham (Kent)	EY-tum
Ilkley	IL-klih
Inverary	in-vuh-RAIR-ih
Jervaulx	*While* JAR-vis *is the old pronunciation it is nowadays called* JER-voh
Keighley (W. Yorks)	KEETH-lih
Keswick	KEZ-zik
Kirkby	*Generally, the* **'k'** *isn't sounded, as in* **Kirkby Lonsdale** *and* **Kirkby Stephen**: KER-bih. *But there are exceptions, like* **Kirkby Mallory**, *Leicestershire, which sound the* **'k'**: KERK-bih
Leicester	LES-ter
Leominster	LEM-ster
Looe	loo
Loughborough	LUF-bruh
Lympne	lim
Malmesbury	MARMS-brih
Malpas	MOH-pus (*in Cornwall*), MAL-pus (*in Gwent*) and MUHL-pus (*in Cheshire*)
Menai Strait	MEN-eye
Meopham (Kent)	MEP-pum
Mousehole (Cornwall)	MOO-zel
Norwich	NOR-idj
Ospringe	OS-prinj
Ottinge	OT-inj
Oundle	OWN-duhl (*to rhyme with* **now**)

Magdalen and Magdalene
While **Magdalen** in Norfolk is pronounced
MAG-dul-lun, the colleges at Oxford
(**Magdalen**) and Cambridge (**Magdalene**)
Universities go a different route; both are
pronounced MORD-lin. To help you remember
this there is a limerick mnemonic:

A doddery old don of Divinity
Made boast of his daughter's virginity.
   They must have been dawdlin'
   Down at old Magdalen –
It couldn't have happened at Trinity.

Pall Mall	pal-mal, *to rhyme with* **shall**, *although there is a tendency for some people to say* pel-mel, *rhyming with* **shell**. **The Mall** *is also pronounced to rhyme with* **shall**, *despite a persistent rumour that it should be pronounced* morl
Pontefract	PON-tih-<u>frakt</u> (PUM-fret *is the old form*)
Reculver	rih-KUL-vuh
Redruth	red-ROOTH
Scilly Isles	SIL-lih
Scone	skoon
Shrewsbury	SHROHZ-brih
Solihull	<u>sol</u>-ih-HUL
Southwark (London)	SUH-thik
Southwick (W. Sussex)	SOW-thwik
Spalding	SPORL-ding
Stiffkey	STIF-kih, *although the archaic form* STYOO-kih *still persists locally*

Stour	stoor (*the river in Kent*); *elsewhere it is mostly* stow-uh (*to rhyme with* **now**)

Teston (Kent)	TEE-suhn
Tideford	TID-ih-fud
Tighnabruaich	ty-nuh-BROO-uk
Tintagel	tin-TAJ-uhl
Tonbridge	TUN-bridj
Towcester	TOH-stuh
Trottiscliffe (Kent)	TROZ-lih

Uist	YOO-ist
Ulgham (Northumberland)	UFF-um
Ulik	YOO-lik
Ulverston	OO-ston
Uttoxeter	yoo-TOKS-ih-tuh

Wednesbury	WENZ-bree
Welwyn Garden City	wel-lin
West Wickham	WIK-um
West Wycombe	WIK-um
Wickhambreaux	WIK-um-broo
Widnes	WID-nis
Woolwich	WOOL-idj
Wrekin, The	REE-kun
Wymondham	WIM-un-dum *in Leicestershire*; WIN-dum *in Norfolk*

Wrestling with Welsh

Although the spelling of Welsh place-names retains its devious purity, Welsh as far as pronunciation goes is a language in transition. North and South Wales disagree on many pronunciations, and there are local variations to contend with as well.

But with Wales a much-visited duchy it's worth trying to get your tongue around some of the places you're likely to encounter. The main problem is to get the hang of the double 'l' (*Ll*). This is expressed by placing your tongue behind your upper teeth and sounding something between a 'k' and an 'h' before the 'l'. This is difficult enough where the 'Ll' is at the beginning of a name like *Llandudno*, but positively diabolical where the 'll' occurs within the name, like *Llangollen* and *Pwllheli*. The sound is indicated here by the symbol (kh).

Abergavenny	<u>ab</u>-uh-gav-EN-ih
Aeronwy	eye-RUN-wih
Beddgelert	beth-GEL-ut
Bettws-y-Coed	BET-us-ih-COY-ed
Builth Wells	bilth wells
Cader Idris	KAD-uh ID-ris
Caerphilly	kuh-FILL-ih
Cefn Mawr	<u>kev</u>-un MOW-uh
Clwyd	KLOO-wid
Criccieth	KRIK-ih-<u>eth</u>
Cwmbran	koom-BRUN
Cwmmawr	koo-MOW-uh (*rhymes with* **now**)
Dduallt	*Virtually impossible for non-Welsh tongues, but* THIH-ulkt *would be an acceptable attempt*
Dinas	DEE-nus
Dolgellau	dol-GE(kh)-lih *or* dol-GETH-lih
Glyn-y-Groes	<u>glih</u>-nuh-GROY-is
Gwynedd	GWIN-uth
Heol-y-Cyw	<u>hay</u>-ul-ah-KYOO
Laugharne	larn
Llandaf	(kh)LAN-daf
Llandoverey	(kh)lan-DUV-rih
Llandrindod Wells	(kh)lan-DRIN-dod

Llandudno	(kh)lan-DID-noh
Llanelli	(kh)lan-ELL-ih

Llanfair-pwllgwyngyll-gogerychwyrndrobwll-llandysilio-gogogoch

(Usually known by its abbreviated version:
Llanfair, Gwynedd)
Thousands of place-names have become the
subject of limericks, and Llanfair is no
exception. The shortened name in the first line
of the following limerick is pronounced (kh)LAN-
vyr-poo(kh)l-gwin-gy(kh)l.

A young man of Llanfair-pwllgwyngyll
While sunbathing nude on the shingle
  Had the whole Eisteddfod
  Shouting 'Oh My Dear God!'
Then they sang some impossible jingle

Llangollen	(kh)lan-GOKH-lan
Llanrwst	(kh)lan-ROOST
Llanthony	(kh)lan-TOH-nih
Llyn Celyn	(kh)<u>loo</u>-in-KEL-in
Maentwrog	myn-TYOO-rog
Nercwys	NAIR-kwis
Penmaen-mawr	pen-min-MOW-uh
Penrhyndeudraeth	<u>pen</u>-rin-DY-drith
Presteigne	pres-TIN
Pwllheli	pooh-(kh)EL-lih
Rhayader	RY-uh-duh

Talachddu	tuh-LAK-thuh
Tal-y-llyn	tal-ih-(kh)LIN
Tan-y-bwlch	tan-ih-BWOOLK
Tanygrisiau	tan-ih-GRIS-yow
Towyn	TOH-win
Yspytty Ifan	US-put-ih IF-un

Don't Let Family Names Fool You

Could you correctly write down the names of persons whose monnikers sounded like *Priducks*, *Wawkup* or *Kahoon*? Perhaps more to the point, could you, having been handed a list of guest names, announce them without giving offence? With names like *de Crespigny*, *Lascelles*, *Rieu* or *Weymss*?

Surnames in the British Isles can be just as contrary as its place-names. Here are a few that could land you in trouble.

Abercrombie	*Can be* ab-er-KRUM-bih *or* ab-er-KROM-bih
Allbeury	uhl-BYOO-rih
Bache	baytch
Bagehot	BAD-jut
Baillieu	BAY-loo
Bevin, Aneurin	uh-NY-rin BEV-un
Bewick, Thomas	BYOO-ik
Blount	blunt
Blyth	bly, *but sometimes* blyth
Bosenquet	BOH-zun-ket
Brough	bruff
Buchanan	buh-KAN-un

85

There Was a Young Man Called Cholmondeley-Colquhoun

Yes, another unlikely limerick! This time the humble poetic form pokes fun at a very old English family name. The Cholmondeleys have been a well-connected family from the time of Charles I, but when you spell your name Cholmondeley and pronounce it **CHUM-lih**, you must expect to provoke some mirth. Like this example, which combines the name with another, equally capricious stable-mate, Colquhoun – pronounced *kuh-HOON*:

A young man called Cholmondeley-Colquhoun
Kept as a pet a babolquhoun.
   His mother said, 'Cholmondeley,
   Do you think it quite colmondeley
To feed your babolquhoun with a spolquhoun?'

Cabot	KAB-ot
Cadogan	kah-DUG-un
Carnegie	kar-NEE-gee, *but also* kar-NAY-gee
Chevenix-Trench	SHEV-en-iks-TRENCH
Chisholm	CHIZ-zum
Cholmondeley	CHUM-lih
Colquhoun	kuh-HOON
Cowper Powys, John	KOOP-er POH-is
Crespigny, de	KREP-nih
Cruikshank	KROOK-shank
Deschamps	DAY-shah(n)
De Soissons	<u>duh</u> SWAR-soh(n)
Devereux	DEV-er-<u>ooks</u>
Drogheda	DROY-ih-dah
Duart	DYOO-art
Duchesne	duh-SHAYN

| Dumaresq | doo-MER-rik |
| Dumas | dyoo-MAR |

Fahey	fay
Farquhar	FAR-kuh, *but also* FAR-kwar
Featherstonehaugh	*Watch this one, because it can be heard as* FETH-uh-ston-<u>hor</u>, FES-ton-<u>hor</u>, FEE-sun-<u>hay</u>, FEER-stun-<u>huh</u> *and* FAN-shor *to name but a few!*

Famous Institutions

Here are some well-known establishments whose pronunciations can be evasive.

Aeolian Hall	ee-OH-lih-an
Alleyn's School	ALL-inz
Balliol College	BAY-lyol
Caius College	keez
Cliveden	KLIV-den
Courtauld Institute	KOH-tohld, *despite the original family pronunciation of* KOR-toh
Geffrye Museum	JEF-rih
Glyndebourne	GLYND-burn
Hallé Orchestra	HAL-ee
Roedean School	ROH-din
Sauchiehall Street	sok-kih-HORL
Savile Club	SAV-il
Madame Tussaud's	tuh-SORDS
Wellesley College	WELS-lih

ffrench-Beytagh	<u>frensh</u>-BIH-tuh
Fiennes, Sir Ranulph	fynz
Finucane	fin-OOH-kun, *but also* fin-YOO- kun
Flaharty	FLAR-uh-<u>tih</u>
Foulds	folds
Foulkes	fohks
Fuchs	fooks
Furneaux	FER-noh
Gerhardie	juh-HAR-dih
Girouard	JIH-roo-<u>ard</u>
Goossens	GOO-suns
Goudge	gooj
Gough	goff
Grosvenor	GROHV-ner
Hakluyt	HAK-lut
Harewood	HAR-wood
Home	hum, *but sometimes* hohm
Ionides	eye-ON-ih-dees
Iveagh, Earl of	EYE-vay
Keightley	KEET-lih
Keough	KEE-oh
Keynes, John Maynard	kayns
Knollys	nohlz
Lafcadio	laf-KAD-yoh
Lamplugh	LAM-ploo
Lascelles	LAS-suls
Le Carré	luh-KAR-<u>ray</u>
Le Fanu	LEE-fuh-<u>noo</u>
Lehmann	LAY-mun
Le Mesurier	<u>luh</u>-MEZ-yuh-ruh
Lisle	Lye, *but also* Lyl
Livesey	LIV-sih
Llewellyn	(kh)lew-WEL-lin

88

Jawbreakers

There are some names that strike fear and terror into the minds of the nation's radio and television newsreaders – newsreaders' nightmares that jump out of a script to induce a paralysing form of airwave anxiety in the unfortunate victim. The following list demonstrates why:

Zbigniew Brzezinski – US political adviser
Vignis Finnbogadottir – President of Iceland
Eddie Niedzwiecki – former Chelsea Club footballer
Maricica Puica – Romanian athlete
Mstislav Rostropovich – great Russian cellist
Gennadiy Rozhdestvensky – Russian conductor
Rev Ndabaningi Sithole – Zimbabwean politician
Murgigesh Sivasithamparam – Indian lawyer
Li Xiannian – President of China
Siobodan Zivojinovic – Yugoslavian tennis player

Lunghi	LUN-gih
Lutyens, Sir Edward	LUT-junz
McAvoy	MAK-ah-<u>voy</u>
McCaughan	muh-KAK-un
McCaughey	muh-KAK-ih
McCrea	muh-KRAY
McElroy	MAK-il-<u>roy</u>
McFadyean	mak-FAD-yun
McGahern	muh-GAK-un
McGee	mah-GEE
McGeough	muh-GOH
MacInerney	*mak-in-ER-nih*

Maclise	muh-KLIS
McMenemey	muk-MEN-uh-<u>mee</u>
Macready	muh-KREE-dih
Maher	mar, *although for some families it's* MAR-uh
Mahon	marn
Mahoney	MAR-uh-nih
Mahony	MAR-nih
Mainwaring	MAN-uh-<u>ring</u>
Margolis	mar-GOH-lis
Margolyes	MAR-guh-<u>lis</u>
Margulies	MAR-goo-<u>lis</u>
Marjoribanks	MARCH-banks
Maugham, Somerset	morm
Menzies, John	MIN-gis

Products and Companies

Some names of products and companies can often be confusing:

Adidas	ah-DEE-das
André Deutsch	AHN-dry DOYTCH
Badedas	BAH-deh-das
Cartier (jewellers)	KAR-tih-ay
Champneys	SHAMP-niz
Cockburns Port	KOH-burns
Coutts bank	kuts, *but sometimes* koots
Fabergé (perfume)	FAB-ah-jay
Gauloise (cigarettes)	GAL-wahr
Glenmorangie (whisky)	glen-muh-RAN-jih
Gollancz (publishers)	goh-LANTS
Ind Coope (brewers)	ind koop
Laphroaig (whisky)	luh-FROYG
Nestlé	NEST-lih
Passat	pah-SAT
Weidenfeld & Nicolson	VY-dun-felt

Meyrick	MEH-rik
Michell	mih-SHEL
Milais	MIL-lay
Molyneux	MOL-ih-noh
Monkton	MUNK-tun
Montagu of Beaulieu	BEW-lih
Mulcahy	mul-KAY-ih
Niklaus	NIK-loh; *also* NIK-lus
O'Flaherty	oh-FLAR-her-<u>tih</u>
Orczy, Baroness	ORT-zih
Pierrepont	PEER-pont
Prideaux	PRID-uks
Prynne	prin
Rhys	*Take your pick from* ris, rees, rys *and even* riss!
Rieu	REE-oh
Ruthven	RIV-un
Sachs	saks
St John	*This name exists in two forms*: SIN-jun (**St John-Stevas, MP**) *and* saynt-JON (*actress* **Jill St John**)
Sandys	Sands
Seth, Vikram (author)	VIK-rum SAYT
Sauvage	SAV-idj
Schofield	SKOH-feeld
Souness	SOO-nes
Strachan	strorn
Strachey	STRAY-kih
Strahan	strorn
Strauss	strows (*to rhyme with* **mouse**)
Suchet	SOO-shay
Synge	sing
Tangye	TANG-gih

Tiarks	TEE-arks
Tissot	TEE-soh
Tollemache	TOL-mash
Tradescant	truh-DES-kant
Trebilcock	treh-BIL-koh
Trefusis	trih-FYOO-sis
Trevelyan	trih-VIL-yan
Trollope	TROL-lop
Tugendhat	TOO-gun-hart
Tuohey	TOO-ih
Twisleton-Wykeham-Feinnes	*see Fiennes*
Tyssen, Baron	TY-sun
Urquart	ER-kart
Ustinov, Peter	YOO-stin-of
Vaughan-Williams	VORN WIL-yams
Vogt	voht
Voigt	voyt
Waldegrave	WOR-grayv, *but now usually* WORL-deh-grayv
Wauchope	WOR-kup
Waugh	wor
Weinstock	WYN-stok
Weymss	weems
Yonge	yung

Know Your Classics

It's surprising how often classical allusions creep into our reading and conversation, so it's useful to know how to pronounce those often perplexing legendary Greek and Roman names.

Achilles	uh-KIL-ees
Aeneas	eh-NEE-us
Aeneid	eh-NEE-id
Aeschylus	ES-kul-lus
Aesop	EE-sop
Agamemnon	ag-ah-MEM-nun
Antigone	an-TIG-uh-nee
Aphrodite	<u>a</u>f-roh-DY-tih
Aristophanes	<u>a</u>r-is-TOF-uh-<u>nees</u>
Artemis	AR-tih-mus
Bellerophon	beh-LER-uh-<u>fon</u>
Canopus	kuh-NOH-pus
Charybdis	kuh-RIB-dis
Cicero	SIS-uh-roh
Circe	SER-see
Cybele	SIB-ih-lee
Daedalus	DED-ul-lus
Dionysus	<u>dy</u>-uh-NY-sus
Endymion	en-DIM-ih-on
Euripides	yoo-RIP-ih-<u>dees</u>
Eurydice	yoo-RID-ih-<u>see</u>
Hades	HAY-dees
Heracles	HER-uh-klees
Hermione	her-MEE-uh-nee
Herodotus	huh-ROD-uh-tus
Hippolyte	hih-POL-ih-tee
Laocoön	lay-OK-oh-on
Livy	LIV-ee
Minotaur	MIN-uh-<u>tor</u>
Odysseus	oh-DIS-ih-us
Oedipus	EE-dip-us

Ovid	OV-id
Persephone	<u>per</u>-SEF-uh-nee
Phaedra	FEE-druh
Plutarch	PLOO-tark
Pyramus	PIR-uh-mus
Scylla	SIL-luh
Silenus	sy-LEE-nus
Sophocles	SOF-uh-<u>klees</u>
Sphinx	sfinks
Terpsichore	terp-SIK-uh-ree
Thebes	theebz
Thucydides	THYOO-sid-uh-<u>dees</u>
Vergil	VER-jil
Xenophone	ZEN-uh-fun
Zeus	zooss

A Final Reminder . . .

Once you've sharpened up your pronunciation skills,
don't stop. If you come across a word or name that
you're not sure how to pronouce, ask around. Libraries
and local radio stations can often help. Here, for
example, are twenty words, terms and names found
in a single issue of *The Sunday Times*. Can you
correctly pronounce them all? Answers on page 96.

Capuchin	_____
Nemesis	_____
Sikh	_____
Pottinger, James	_____

Bosnia-Herzegovina _____

Saudi _____

Byzantine _____

Elwes _____

Gruyère cheese _____

Phoebe _____

Cymric _____

Cognac _____

Arkansas _____

Bauhaus _____

Haydn _____

Lyons (France) _____

Philistine _____

Quirinal _____

sauté _____

Uranus _____

Answers to Tests and Puzzles

Perverse Pronunciation (Page 51)	The pronunciation of **MNOMNOUPTE** to make a common six-letter word is:

M MN as in *autumn*
I O as in *women*
N MN as in *mnemonics*
U OU as in *tough*
T PT as in *ptarmigan*
E E as in *hare*

Make a Choice (Page 76)	The correct choices are: *lon-JEV-ih-tee, ik-STEM-pree, moh-HEE-kun, KIB-bits* and *OH-dyum*.

A Spell at Games (Page 76)	The pronunciations are: *BAK-uh-ruh, BAK-gam-un, bih-ZEEK, bool, shuh-MAN-duh-FAYR, KROH-kay, YOO-kuh, hy-ly, pih-KAY, va(h)n-ay-er(h)n.*
Medical Matters (Page 76)	The accepted pronunciations are: *KOL-uh-jen, EN-doh-kryn, en-DOSK-uh-pee, you-STAY-shun, jin-jih-VY-tus, HIS-tuh-meen, in-truh-VEE-nus, in-VEE-troh, lap-ah-ROS-kuh-pee, ok-SIP-ih-tuhl, per-ih-STAL-sis, pluh-SEE-boh.*
Occupations (Page 77)	The correct choices are: *an-EESS-thuh-tist, AN-tik-war-ee, ar-TIF-is-er, SHOH-fuh* is preferred, *kon-TROLL-er, gy-nuh-KOL-uh-jist, orth-oh-PEE-dist, som-UHL-yay.*
Music to the Ear (Page 77)	*an-TIF-uh-nee, ar-PEJ-ih-oh, BAR-kuh-rohl, AY-tyood, im-prov-ih-ZAY-shun, pit-zih-KAR-toh, toot-ih, vih-BRAR-toh.*
A Final Reminder . . . (Page 94)	*KAP-yoo-shin, NEM-ih-sis, seek, POT-tin-jer, BOZ-nih-uh hertz-oh-GOV-ih-nuh, SOW-dih, bih-ZAN-tyn, EL-wiz, GROO-yehr, FEE-bee, KIM-rik, KON-yak, AR-kun-sor, BOW-hows* (rhymes with *now*), *HY-duhn, LEE-ohr(n) FIL-ih-styn, KWIH-rin-uhl, SOH-tay, yoor-RAY-nus* – although in astronomical circles it is pronounced *YOOR-ah-nus.*